HOW tO be

DISABLED
and
PROUD

PUFFIN BOOKS

UK | USA | Canada | Ireland | Australia
India | New Zealand | South Africa

Puffin Books is part of the Penguin Random House group of companies
whose addresses can be found at global.penguinrandomhouse.com.

www.penguin.co.uk   www.puffin.co.uk   www.ladybird.co.uk

First published 2025
001

Text copyright © Cathy Reay, 2025
Illustrations copyright © Jaleel Hudson, 2025
The moral right of the author/illustrator has been asserted

Set in Museo Slab Rounded 10.5pt/17pt by Mandy Norman
Printed in Great Britain by Clays Ltd, Elcograf S.p.A

The authorized representative in the EEA is Penguin Random House Ireland,
Morrison Chambers, 32 Nassau Street, Dublin D02 YH68
A CIP catalogue record for this book is available from the British Library

ISBN: 978-0-241-67696-7

All correspondence to:
Puffin Books
Penguin Random House Children's
One Embassy Gardens, 8 Viaduct Gardens, London SW11 7BW

A CIP catalogue record for this book is available from the British Library

HOW TO BE DiSABLED and PROUD

CATHY REAY

Illustrated by Jaleel Hudson

PUFFIN

For Mariama and Isatou

CONTENTS

INTRODUCTION

A bit about me – and who I wrote this book for

Have you ever felt like you don't fit in anywhere?

Or as though no-one understands what it feels like to be you?

Maybe you feel like the only person in the whole wide world who looks, moves or thinks the way you do.

Well, I'm here to tell you that you are NOT alone and that **you belong in this world exactly as you are.**

Hi! My name is Cathy, I'm a mum, a writer and editor, and I live in England. I'm creative, sometimes a bit silly, and I have an amazing group of friends. Another thing about me is that I have a disability called achondroplasia. I know – that word is kinda tough to remember. You say it like *ay-kon-dro-play-see-ah* . . . An easier word you might already know is **dwarfism**. Achondroplasia is a type of dwarfism.

Having achondroplasia dwarfism means my arms, legs, fingers and toes are shorter compared to most other people's; my head is bigger and heavier; and my spine (that long bone in the middle of our backs) is curved. I can run around, play games, work, learn and have fun just like anyone else, but *how* I do those things is different to how others do them. For example, I run very slowly and I get tired easily. I hold a pen and my knife and fork differently to most people. When I was a kid, I fell over a lot, and for most of my childhood I needed someone to help me with my underwear so I could go for a wee.

Maybe you do some things differently to other kids too? Perhaps you sometimes find it tricky asking for help when you need it, or maybe you just need a reminder that it's *kinda sorta okay* if you're not the best at running/sports/maths/drawing or anything else that you might find hard sometimes.

Whatever the reason you're reading this, I'm here to help! I wrote this book just for you. Well, technically, I wrote it for both of us, because young Cathy needed this then just as much as you probably do now (and maybe even more).

When I was young, there weren't really any books written for kids like me. My whole world was so much taller than I was – my parents, family and friends were all average height, except one friend who lived very far away. And this was before we could communicate through WhatsApp!

I never saw people like me on TV either – most of the musicians and actors I loved weren't disabled. And when disabled people were on the screen – like the super-

cool rock singer Ian Dury – non-disabled people would often react like,

"OMG-AMAZING!"

Sorta like, wow, he can sing *even though* he's disabled. And there was me thinking, of course he can – his disability doesn't affect his ability to sing!

Back then, disabled people were either seen as these amazing heroes because we could sing/dance/run/act/[insert any other activity here], or people just felt sorry for us.

To me, it always felt really *weird* when people said I was amazing just for being disabled and living my life. And I didn't like it when people felt sorry for me either. To be honest, I often wished people would stop commenting on and thinking about what I looked like or what I could do altogether.

A lot has changed since I was a kid, and nowadays there are so many disabled actors, singers, writers, TV presenters, models and athletes on our screens, and in books and magazines. Laws have changed, making it easier for disabled people to have jobs whether they're famous or not. There are more disabled doctors, dentists, hairdressers, shopkeepers, bankers, and every other type of job. The more we see disabled people represented in everyday life, the more likely it is that non-disabled people will treat us just like anybody else – and not be so surprised to see us out in the world. But society still has a long way to go towards fully accepting all disabled people, which we'll talk more about later in this book.

As a young person, I often felt like life was so much easier for other kids. They could find cute shoes that fit their feet. They won swimming certificates and sports day medals all the time (or at least, it felt that way). When they stood up in class, they were still able to see the teacher **AND** they didn't have to deal with people making constant judgements about them and their disabilities.

On top of all that, I was sometimes teased and bullied by other children who were afraid of the way I looked or who just didn't like seeing someone like me. Dealing with bullies was definitely the hardest part of growing up, and the part where I felt most alone. Sometimes I really wanted a friend to talk to about it, or who would support me in the playground. I wanted some advice on what I could do when people were being unkind. And I really wanted friends that liked me for who I was, and who could tell me that the mean things the bullies said just weren't true. If you're experiencing anything like this, I want you to know that a lot of kids go through similar things, and that being bullied is never, ever your fault.

As I've gotten older, I've built amazing friendships, travelled the world, and done so many incredible things with my life. I've been to university and even worked in another country. I've fallen in (and out of!) love, been married, become a mum, adopted animals, had jobs I enjoy, and I've bought a house all on my own (okay, a flat. But it's a start!). I've campaigned for the rights of disabled people worldwide, and met so many awesome people along the way. The difficulties that I've faced have only made me stronger and more determined. **I know I belong in this world exactly as I am, and I want you to know it too.**

Maybe you have been through some of the same things as me. Maybe you don't feel like you fit in, or you've been made to feel unwelcome by other kids. Maybe you struggle making friends or doing sports or other lessons, in ways that other kids don't. Of course, not every disabled kid will go through all the same stuff, but a lot of the experiences discussed in these pages may be similar to yours. I've got a few of my fab disabled friends to share some of their experiences too.

I hope this book helps you to feel understood and to know that you are not alone. I hope it helps you to see that lots of us find things hard, and that it's okay to need support. I hope it helps you find people who understand and celebrate you for who you are. And I hope it reminds you that, no matter what you can or cannot do,

You are a brilliant, wonderful person and you belong in this world exactly the way you are.

Oh, and by the way, before we go any further, I should probably tell you that **'disabled' is not a bad word**. I know, you're thinking, 'huh'? But it's true. Being disabled gives me an understanding of the world that is special and beautiful and rare. It helps me to appreciate that we're all awesome, no matter what we look like or what we can or can't do – **AND** being disabled can be really fun and exciting too, as you'll find out later in the book.

After all, wouldn't life be really boring if we all looked, felt and behaved the same way?

NOTE TO PARENTS AND CAREGIVERS

(HEY KIDS! You can skip this bit and head to Chapter 1)

Firstly, I want to say thank you. Thank you for raising such a brilliant kid and having these conversations about disability with them from early on, which will help to ensure they also turn into an incredible, assertive, self-assured adult. Raising children is a blessing (when they're not driving us up the wall, that is), and as a mum of two I know those highs and the lows very well!

Parents of disabled children rarely get recognition for how different our parenting journey can be. I have often experienced the jarring feeling of in one way being part of a supportive parenting network, while in another sense, knowing my place within it is on the periphery, never fully accepted or understood by others in the parenting community.

The alienation that I sometimes experience in parenthood is in part because my kids are disabled, but it is also because *I'm* disabled. People don't

know what to do about them or me, or they just want to pretend we don't exist. Maybe you've experienced some of that loneliness and isolation too. Maybe you haven't known where to go for support or how to equip your kid with the tools they need to navigate the many barriers they'll face. Maybe you've had to deal with intrusive questions at drop off and pick up, and maybe you're struggling with unlearning the things the world has told you about disability that just aren't true.

I hope that you and your kid(s) have the support you need. But, just in case you need a little bit of extra help and guidance, this is the book for your family. I'm here to teach your awesome kids that they are not the problem and that their disabilities are not something to be fixed or to be ashamed of. This book will teach them about ableism and inaccessibility in a relatable way and show them how it's up to society – not disabled people – to remove the barriers that we face. But in the same breath, it will teach them some of the things that we can do to make life just a little bit easier for ourselves. This book will give your children tools to navigate systems that aren't built for them, and encourage them to ask for help – often with you alongside them! It'll show them how to use their voice to advocate for change, how to be comfortable in their disabled identity and maybe even a bit proud too. And there's a list of further reading and resources at the end to support what they're learning in this book.

There are bits in here that might be hard for your kid (or you, or both!) to read or accept, and there are bits that might feel overwhelming too. Some parts – like speaking up in meetings about their care or organizing support – they will almost definitely need your help with (at least to start with). I encourage you to read this book too, and to come back to it whenever you need guidance discussing any of the themes it covers. This is their journey, but they're going to need your support (with their consent of course).

Unlike some disabled kids, yours will already know they're not alone simply because they have you – a parent or carer that accepts and loves them and is willing to put in the work to help them navigate this complex and sometimes unkind world. Thank you for sharing this book with them, and for understanding that helping your child learn about and be comfortable in their disabled identity is so important.

They'll thank you when they're ready too.

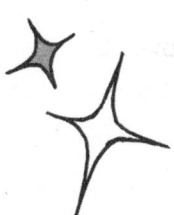

The term **disability** or **disabled** includes so many different impairments and types of impairment, and I'm aware that not all disabled kids will be able to read this book, process its contents or take the actions suggested in its pages. This is also why I've written it with you, the parent or carer, in mind. I hope that some of the advice and information I've shared here will be helpful for you too.

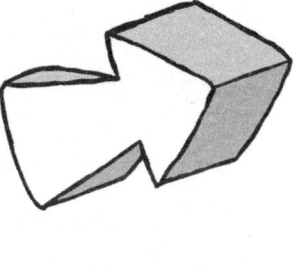

CHAPTER 1

Am I Even Disabled Anyway?

Woah, we're diving straight in with the tough questions! Disabled is a big word, isn't it? But is it a positive word or a negative word? Who is allowed to call themselves disabled and who isn't? Will people think you're weird for saying you're disabled? (*Can we even say that word, or should we just say it in a really quiet voice?*)

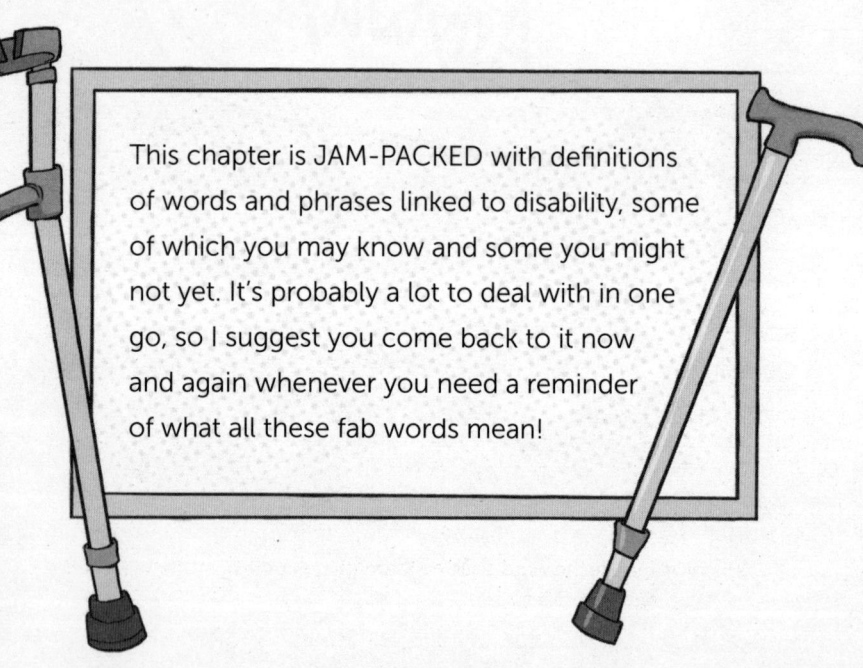

Here's the good news – you can absolutely call yourself disabled if you want to. It's not wrong, and it's not bad. In this chapter we're going to explore what exactly that word means, as well as unpacking some of the other words you might have heard people use around disability, such as ableism and inaccessibility.

This chapter is JAM-PACKED with definitions of words and phrases linked to disability, some of which you may know and some you might not yet. It's probably a lot to deal with in one go, so I suggest you come back to it now and again whenever you need a reminder of what all these fab words mean!

Before that though, I'd like you to remember something:

The way you describe yourself is totally, utterly, completely up to <u>you.</u>

Nobody else. Not your family, friends or school. Not other disabled people – not even me[1], the person writing this book. If you don't want to call yourself disabled, no problem. If you prefer using another term, or maybe nothing at all, that's your choice. And it's also okay for you to change your mind whenever you want and however many times you want. Nobody else has the power to decide what or who you are or how you describe yourself. EVER.

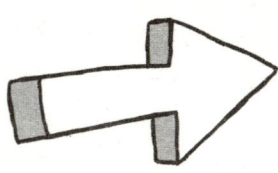

---

[1] I will, however, use the word disabled through this book to mean people like you and me – because it's the word I prefer to use.

All I ask is that you read this chapter and have a think about how you'd like to talk about your brain and body. I'm really sorry, but this does involve a bit of a history lesson (I'll make it quick, promise).

A KINDA, SORTA QUICK HISTORY OF THE WORD DISABLED

The word disabled has been around since way before you or I were born, or our parents, or even our grandparents. In fact, the earliest recorded use was in the 1500s, but not in a kind way. Then, in the early 1900s (still a very long time ago), people started using the term handicapped in games and sports to mean something of less value than something else. This slowly made its way into general language to also describe people like you and me. But we're not less valuable than anyone else, are we? NO WAY!

Nowadays, people don't really say handicapped (well, unless someone is trying to be mean). After all, the reason we struggle sometimes isn't because there's something *wrong* with us – it's because our bodies and/or brains work differently, and all that means is we might need some extra help from time to time or to do things in a different way.

Fast-forward to today and many people – including our governments and world leaders – use the word disabled again, only with a much more empowering and positive meaning than it did before. Today, the word disabled doesn't mean that someone is less important or imperfect; in fact, for many people the word represents an identity to be proud of. Disability isn't something to be ashamed of, and if someone thinks being disabled is bad, that's usually because they feel ableism towards us – and that's likely because they've been taught things about disability that just aren't true.

What is ableism?

Ableism means prejudice and discrimination towards disabled people. You might now be thinking, hold on, what's the difference between prejudice and discrimination?

Prejudice: holding certain beliefs about a person based on their characteristics, and in this case, that characteristic is their disability – for example, disabled people can't work.

Some people are more ableist than others, but everyone is ableist sometimes – even disabled people! Ableism focuses on disability as the problem, rather than looking at all the ways in which society is failing disabled people. Like not giving someone a job because you think their disability means they can't work, instead of looking at how the workplace could be changed to make it possible for them to work there. It's much easier to say the reason that person can't work there is because they're disabled, rather than to try and fix the workplace for them. But just because it's easier to say that, doesn't make it true.

There are many barriers (things that make it harder to do something) in society that create problems for disabled people. Barriers can be visible – like steps to a building without a ramp – or invisible, like not allowing someone to work different hours. These barriers put pressure on disabled people to deal with these kinds of problems by themselves, when actually it should be up to everyone to make society more inclusive.

We're going to discuss all of this in more detail as we go through this book, but for now all I want you to know that **your disability isn't the problem – ableism is!**

A quick note on intersectionality

Intersectionality was defined by the civil rights activist, writer and law professor Kimberlé Crenshaw in 1989 as a way of explaining the many things that make up who we are, which could include disability, race, gender, sexuality, class, nationality, education and other things.

Discrimination can be experienced by people based on one or multiple parts of their identity. For example, as a white disabled person, I am sometimes treated badly because of the way people think about my disability. But I am not treated badly because I'm white, whereas a disabled person who isn't white might be treated badly because of someone's beliefs about their disability *and* their race.

My friend Jameisha is Black and disabled, and says:

> *We all have a different story; there is no one disabled experience, but we should also recognize there are parts of our identity – whether that's race, gender, or anything else – that impact the way our disabilities are experienced. Recognizing intersectionality is so important when we're talking about the discrimination we face in the disabled community. It also allows us to work together to make a world that's more inclusive for **all** disabled people.*

How about you – does your identity meet different intersections? Which ones are they?

We'll come back to intersectionality later on in Chapter 6, but for now it's useful to know what this word means and why it's important when talking about disabled people's experiences.

DISABLED PERSON VS PERSON WITH A DISABILITY

While the word disabled on its own is now used by more and more people to describe themselves, some of us refer to ourselves as a **disabled person** or as a **person with a disability** (or a **person with disabilities).**

For me, calling myself a disabled person feels empowering. Being disabled isn't the only thing about me and who I am as a person, but it does affect everything I experience, so I think it should be the first word. I don't want to shy away from it.

Some people prefer to use person with a disability because they want to be recognized as a person first, and disabled second. And that's totally okay too.

Neither term is incorrect – it's a personal choice. Which do you prefer?

Other (less useful) words for disabled

Some people don't like to use the word disabled at all, and there are other words that are sometimes used to describe our community. Maybe you've come across or even used these words before:

⭐ differently abled
⭐ unique
⭐ special
⭐ different/difference

The thing about using words like 'unique', 'different' and 'special' to describe disabled people is that they ignore all the challenges and barriers we face – which are created by the society we live in – and instead focus on how our bodies and brains aren't the same as everyone else's (and anyway, surely *everyone* is different, unique and special?). These words can also feel a bit patronizing sometimes, as though we're being treated like babies.

One of my teachers at primary school used to call me special all the time and I hated it, but I never said anything because well, she said it in a way that made it sound nice, even though it didn't make me feel very nice. When she said it, it sounded like a compliment, but I felt like she was patronizing and othering me from the rest of the class.

Othering: when you other someone, you treat them like they're not part of your group because they're different in some way. This can be experienced by anyone, but it can happen to disabled kids quite a bit. Have other kids ever made you feel like that?

I was lucky to grow up in a family who used the word disabled and didn't feel any shame around it. Because of that, I have always been okay with calling myself disabled. I have also always been happy to tell people that I have dwarfism. If other people made fun of the words I used or had an issue with them, I knew that was their problem, not mine.

Words like 'special', 'different' and 'unique' don't make me feel good. They make me feel a sense of shame, whereas calling myself disabled feels like I have the power over defining what and who I am, and not being ashamed of it. My body IS disabled (which is okay!), and I am disabled by the world around me too (which is not okay!).

I use disabled to describe myself, along with lots of other words, like white, woman, mother, writer and peanut-butter lover! These are all words – not bad, not good, just neutral – for all the different parts that make up who I am.

Learning disabilities

Learning disabilities (or intellectual disabilities) affect your brain and how you learn. They are life-long and can affect activities like reading, doing tests and communicating with others. Dyslexia, dyscalculia and Down syndrome are examples of learning disabilities.

Neurological and neurodevelopmental disabilities

These are disabilities that affect your brain, spinal cord and/or nerves. They can affect how you feel and connect with the world. Examples include autism, ADHD and epilepsy.

Physical disabilities

Physical disabilities can affect your body or parts of your body, its strength, and the way it moves and does things. Dwarfism, blindness and epilepsy are examples of physical disabilities.

Chronic illnesses

Chronic illnesses are long-term health conditions that limit your everyday life and/or mean you need extra medical support. Alzeimer's, cancer and ME/CFS are examples of chronic illnesses.

Some people's disabilities fall into more than one of the above categories (like epilepsy), or you could have a mix of different types of disabilities.

Sometimes people with one disability are more likely to also have another, e.g. people with ADHD are more likely to be dyslexic and/or dyspraxic.

A note about special needs

In the UK, special needs is a term that is generally considered an unkind and outdated way of describing people who have learning disabilities.

But, special educational needs (SEN) is still used when talking about disabled children that require extra support in school.

APPARENT VS NON-APPARENT DISABILITIES (INVISIBLE VS VISIBLE DISABILITIES)

Society often makes sense of people's disabilities by putting them in one of two groups: invisible and visible. Dwarfism is considered a visible disability because you can see it. People who are wheelchair users, have limb loss or cerebral palsy are also considered to be examples of people who have visible disabilities.

Invisible disability is a term used to describe impairments we cannot obviously 'see', such as some chronic illnesses, brain injuries, autism, ADHD or fatigue. However, disability can be much more complicated than these categorizations.

 Many people have more than one disability, and they are sometimes a mix of visible and invisible. For example, someone whose legs don't work and uses a wheelchair – a very visible mobility aid – may also have chronic fatigue, which is not something you can easily see.

 **Mobility Aid:** something you use to help you move around, such as a wheelchair, cane or crutches.

★ Seeing a disability isn't the only way to make sense of it – for example, Blind and visually impaired people can understand disabilities without seeing them.

★ Some disabilities are only visible some of the time.

★ Sometimes a disability is only visible if you know how to look for it.

★ The term 'visible disability' suggests that because we can see the disability, we understand it – but often we don't, whether it's visible or invisible! People might see that I have dwarfism, but that doesn't mean they understand all the ways my life is different to theirs.

★ Categorizing disabilities as visible and invisible can make it seem as though invisible disabilities are somehow less important – which is totally untrue.

For all those reasons, I prefer to say I have a physical or an apparent disability, rather than a visible one. **How about you?**

Non-apparent disabilities

People with non-apparent disabilities have just as much right to call themselves disabled as those whose disabilities are more obvious. If you have a disability that people don't recognize, I want you to know that you are AMAZING and an incredibly welcome and important part of our wonderful disabled community.

Ellie Middleton is autistic and often mistaken for someone who isn't disabled – she didn't realize she was disabled, in fact, until she was an adult. She told me:

> *It can be tricky to know where to start with finding your place in the disabled community when you've grown up not knowing that you were disabled and when your disability isn't easy to spot by the people around you.*

Ellie wears a green sunflower lanyard round her neck, which represents having non-apparent disabilities. It's a clear way for her to show others she is part of the disabled community.

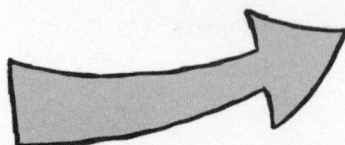

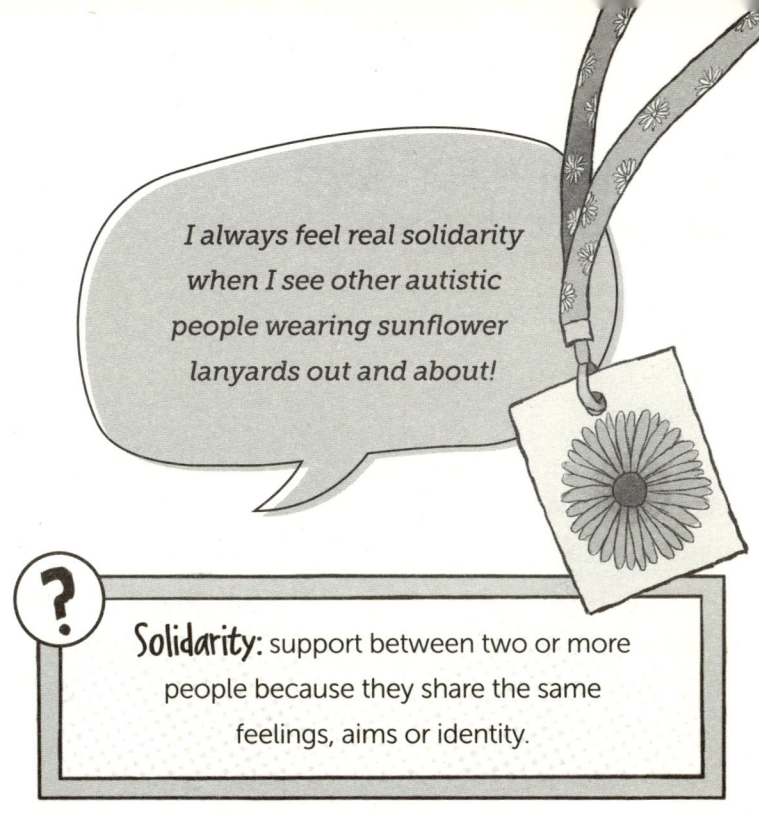

> *I always feel real solidarity when I see other autistic people wearing sunflower lanyards out and about!*

? **Solidarity:** support between two or more people because they share the same feelings, aims or identity.

Ellie also had some really encouraging words for anyone who feels like they're not good enough:

> *Just because you do things differently, doesn't mean that you're wrong, or broken, or damaged. Difference is exactly that – just different! – and it's a natural part of being a human.*
>
> *The things that make us different are the things that make us unique, and 'us' – and that is something to celebrate!*

ACCESSIBILITY AND INACCESSIBILITY

Something else you might hear a lot in relation to disability is whether somewhere or something is accessible.

If something is accessible to us, it means we can access, experience or use it, just like anyone else. *How* we access it might look a little different, though – for example, by using a ramp or lift instead of stairs to enter a building, or using a screen reader to understand a text.

Something being inaccessible means – you guessed it – the opposite. It's when we can't access something, usually because the support we need isn't in place. For example, there's no ramp or lift to the entrance, or the website we are reading is inaccessible to screen readers. Remember earlier when we talked about the different barriers faced by disabled people? Inaccessibility is just another way of describing those barriers.

When we think of something being inaccessible, it's often because disabled people – and specifically often wheelchair users – can't access it. But inaccessibility doesn't just affect disabled people. Barriers to work, education, services and fun things also exist for other people for lots of different reasons. For example:

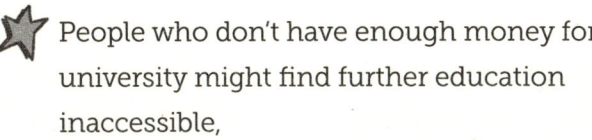 People who don't have enough money for university might find further education inaccessible,

people who are caregivers might struggle to go to an evening dance class,

and some fat people[2] might not be able to find clothes they really love that fit them.

Unfortunately we live in a society where inaccessibility is all around us. We talked earlier about the ableist view that disability is a problem, and inaccessibility is part of this.

When someone can't access something, ableism says that's because there's something wrong with the person or they're not working hard enough. But actually, it's because the thing they're trying to access is inaccessible, which isn't their fault at all!

Buildings, public transport systems, parks, playgrounds and pretty much any public environment you can think of are sadly

2. Just like disabled, fat isn't a bad word – it's a neutral descriptor.

often inaccessible for lots of people for different reasons. Accessible design removes that problem and makes something easier to access for everyone. For example, a playground that has slides and swings of different heights, equipment with extra grips, roundabouts that are wheelchair accessible, and quiet spaces for relaxation can be enjoyed by all children, whether they're disabled or non-disabled.

As disabled people we can often feel like the world isn't built for us, but it doesn't have to be that way. There are ways to build with accessibility in mind from the start – and there are ways to fix things that already exist to make them accessible to more people.

THE MEDICAL MODEL AND THE SOCIAL MODEL

Okay, we're getting into some big words and ideas now, and here are two of the biggest of the book (I think). We're going to look at the two main ways of explaining disability in society – these are called the medical model and the social model.

The medical model

The medical model of disability says that the way our bodies are – like being in pain or having a broken leg – makes our lives more challenging. It sees our bodies as the problem, and not the world around us. The medical model focuses on finding fixes and cures for our bodies.

The social model

The social model of disability is used to describe how things that happen outside of our bodies – like people being unkind and the world not being accessible – make our lives more challenging. It sees society as the problem. The social model focuses on trying to educate the world and make it a more inclusive place.

Over the page are a couple of examples of how each model works in the real world:

SITUATION 1

Someone who is Deaf cannot hear what is happening in a movie they are watching.

A medical model solution:

let's try to fix the person's hearing so they can hear the film.

A social model solution:

let's make the film accessible by adding subtitles, or a sign language interpreter, so they can understand and enjoy the film.

SITUATION 2

A child who has autism cannot sit still for an entire class assembly.

A medical model solution:

let's do everything we can to make the child sit still and they will eventually learn this skill.

A social model solution:

let's relax the rules about sitting still and make the environment more inclusive – maybe by providing a quiet corner, fidget toys and the opportunity to come in and out of the room as they need to.

The medical model focuses on fixing the person, which links back to society's (totally false) view of disability as a problem, whereas the social model focuses on fixing the environment so the person can access what they need.

I like the social model of disability, because I know the world isn't built for people like me, and **I know that's not my fault**. I don't think my body is to blame, and I don't want to change it in order to be more like other people.

I don't think I need fixing, and I don't think you do either.

Not everyone feels the same way as I do about disability. Our feelings about our identity can be complicated, and they can change over time. I asked a couple of my disabled friends for their thoughts on the medical model and the social model. My friend Nina has an apparent disability like me, and she told me:

I'm a writer and a mum of four kids (one who has the same disability as me), and I make silly little videos about disability on the internet. I grew up thinking 'disabled' was a bad word and a bad thing to be. The medical model taught me to think that I was the problem, but then I found the amazing disabled community online and learned about the social model of disability. It was the first time I realized that my legs weren't the problem (my wheelchair fixed that) – the problem was our inaccessible society with its lack of ramps and way too many stairs!

Unlike Nina and I, Jameisha – who we heard from earlier in the chapter – has disabilities that are less apparent, and a very different experience of being disabled.

> *I'm a disabled filmmaker with lupus, which means I experience pain in my joints and get tired very easily. I hold so much pride in being a disabled person and a lot of that is because I view the world through the social model of disability. But as a person with a chronic illness, it's difficult to completely ignore the medical model. My disability is connected to a disease that changes all the time and which causes me pain and fatigue that I have no control over. So, for me it is complex – I feel pride for being disabled but I also know that if a doctor offered me a 'solution' to make my pain go away, I'd accept it.*

How you feel about your disability is completely up to you, and it's okay to feel frustrated by your environment *and* your body or brain sometimes. Something Jameisha, Nina and I all really agree on is that inaccessibility isn't our fault. **It can be empowering to realize that WE are not the problem – a lot of the issues that we face as disabled people simply wouldn't exist if the outside world was more accessible to us.**

Here are just three of the many things that prevent me from doing things I want to:

1 Height restrictions on rollercoasters (Okay, this issue doesn't come up very often, but it's a big one for me. I'm 38 – I want to go on all the scary rides!)

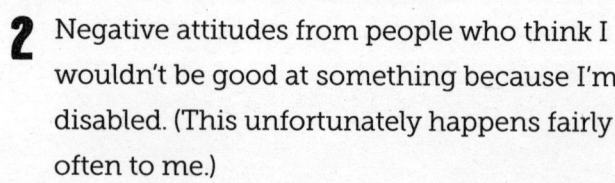

2 Negative attitudes from people who think I wouldn't be good at something because I'm disabled. (This unfortunately happens fairly often to me.)

3 Events where there is no seating for me to be able to rest my legs when I need to (and train stations, bus stops ... there's a lot of spaces with nowhere to sit down!).

It can be
empowering
to realize that
WE are
not the
problem,
society is

You might be disabled by some of these things too. Or maybe for you it's the lack of level access into a building when there's no lift, or the school canteen not having a quiet space for you to be in, or a lack of audio description in a cinema ... or some other stuff entirely. People can be disabled by all kinds of different things.

You can write down some of the things you're disabled by here if you like:

I'm disabled by . . .

_____

_____

_____

_____

_____

_____

While there is still a ton of inaccessibility across the world, many things are slowly becoming *more* accessible too. For example, there are loads more lifts, escalators and ramps where there weren't any before, subtitles on most television programmes and FIDGET toys! These were originally used by neurodivergent people who sometimes need something to help them to feel calm in situations they find stressful or difficult. Nowadays, fidget toys are used by loads of kids – disabled and non-disabled.

But there's still loads of work to be done to make the world truly accessible for all of us. (Turn to Chapter 8 to read more about how all of us can become activists for change!)

Okay, we're almost at the end of this bumper chapter filled with lots of different ways to describe and think about being disabled. Next we're going to talk about family – but before we move on, **the main lessons I want you to take away from this chapter are...**

'Disabled' isn't a bad word. It's just a word that describes part of someone's identity.

 You are not a problem because your body and/or brain works differently to other people's.

 Only you can decide how you want to describe yourself, and you can change your mind at any time if you want to.

 There are lots of people in the disabled community, and **we are all different** in how we think and feel about ourselves.

 The most important thing is that you feel confident and comfortable in who you are and how your body and brain work. And that's what this book is here to help you with!

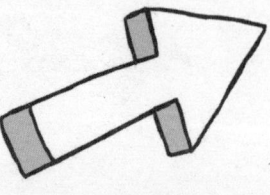

CHAPTER 2

Family Matters

Your family isn't always just the two people that created you – it might be carers, foster parents, adoptive parents, siblings, grandparents, other family members or even close friends. I grew up in a house with my mum and my dad, and I am kinda sorta an only child. Now you might be thinking, *hang on, what does that mean?* Well, I do have a brother and a sister, and when I was a kid they came to stay with us every other weekend, but we've never lived in the same house. That's because my brother and sister have a different mum to me and they lived with her, so they used to visit me, our dad and my mum on weekends. My mum, dad, brother and sister are all non-disabled. Oh and I had a cat, and my mum had a dog.

Hold on, I think I need to draw this:

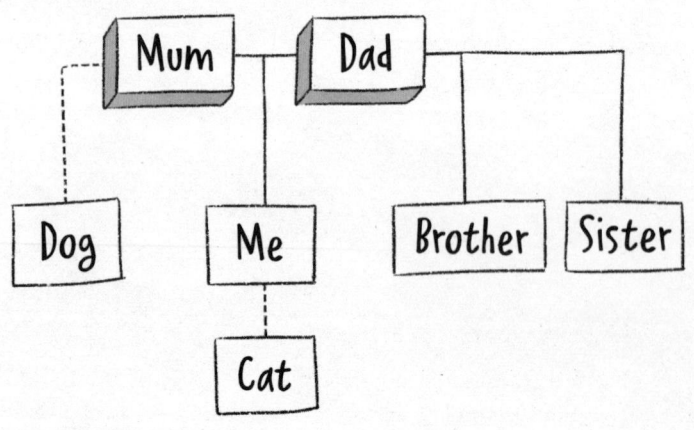

There, that's my family tree from when I was roughly the same age you are now.

What does your family tree look like? Is anyone in your family disabled like you? Maybe they're disabled in a different way, or maybe not at all?

Draw it here, if you want:

In this chapter, we're going to hear from different disabled people about their families. We'll also talk about useful stuff – like how to speak to family members about your support needs – and fun stuff, like who in your family you can really be yourself with and have a laugh. But first, we're going to hear from my good friend Ivy about her experience growing up with one disabled and one non-disabled parent. Ivy has the same type of dwarfism as me and she's actually my oldest friend – we've known each other since we were babies! Here's what she had to say about family:

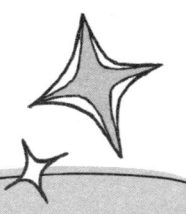

I always felt weirdly lucky as a young person to have separated parents and two very different experiences. For half the week, I lived with my non-disabled mum, stepdad and sisters, and the other half of the week with my dad, who has dwarfism like I do. This meant I grew up with a living example of just what my life could be like when I was an adult. I knew that I could drive, be successful at work, and have friends and a family if I wanted because my dad and grandad had already done it. My amazing mum supported me through my struggles with feeling different, receiving negative attention and being worried about not having teen romances. But by being part of a family with people who looked like me, a lot of those barriers were immediately broken down.

Ivy's dad and grandad were really important role models for her when she was young, as they showed her that she could achieve so many different things. If you have a disabled parent or family member, perhaps you feel the same way? Or maybe you have someone you can identify with who isn't a part of your family? As I was the first person in my family with dwarfism, friends like Ivy have always been super important to me, because when I was growing up, I could ask and share things with her that she understood more than anyone else.

Around 80 per cent of people who have my type of dwarfism (do you remember what it's called? Achondroplasia!) are born into families that are average height, so it's actually super common for people with my disability to be the first – and sometimes the only – person to have it in their families. Being the first person in my family to have dwarfism was a positive experience for me in some ways, but it was sometimes challenging too. I was really lucky to have parents who loved and accepted me for who I was as soon as I was born, and who worked really hard to try to ensure I had a happy childhood and that I was treated fairly.

But like any other parents or caregivers, my parents were only human, and they didn't get parenting right all the time. They could be a bit over the top sometimes – like still wanting to hold my hand when we crossed the road, even when none of my friends were still doing that.

They wanted to make sure I didn't get hurt by the big bad world, but the thing is, it's impossible for anyone to protect us from everything. I kinda sorta think we need to know what's out there waiting for us – both the good and the bad. Otherwise how will we know what to do when we're stuck in a difficult situation?

Have you ever felt annoyed by your parents or caregivers being a bit overprotective? This is totally normal, and it's okay to (kindly) let the adults in your life know if they're being a bit . . . much. In fact, we're going to look at how to talk about this sort of thing with your family in the next section.

While my friend Ivy and I had different experiences growing up – her with her one disabled and one non-disabled parent, me with my two non-disabled parents – we were both lucky enough to have families who loved and accepted us the way we were. Whatever your own family set-up is, the most important thing is that you feel supported and loved (even if you find your adults mega-embarrassing now and again).

TALKING TO FAMILY (AND OTHER GROWN-UPS) ABOUT DISABILITY

Do you find it easy to speak to your family about your disability? Have you ever felt like they don't really understand your disabled identity, or do they seem to get it? Maybe there are people in your wider family – like aunts, uncles or grandparents – who don't always know how to support you in the right way. Or perhaps, like mine were, your adults can be a bit overprotective at times and you wish you had a bit more independence.

If you feel like a family member could be doing more to support you or if you want them to support you in a different way, the best thing to do is talk to them about it or get someone else to speak to them on your behalf. This doesn't just apply to family members either – the same goes for all the grown-ups in your life, such as teachers and doctors (who we'll talk more about in Chapters 4 and 7).

Adults often think they know best, and it can be hard when you're young to have the confidence to let them know when they've got something wrong. Sometimes an adult will be trying to help you, but they are just going about it in the wrong way or not asking what you'd like them to do. Before you try talking to that person, it can be useful to have a think about the things grown-ups can do that are helpful, compared to the things that aren't – and then maybe gently ask them to do the helpful things you need! Over the page are few examples:

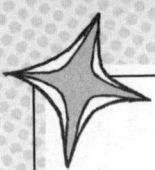

Helpful things grown-ups can do:

✓ Listen to you when you share your needs.

✓ Suggest solutions for problems if they can.

✓ Help you find the solution that is best for you.

✓ Ask you questions if they're unclear on something or need more information.

✓ Be patient and kind, and not make you feel bad asking for anything.

✓ Discuss decisions about your care with you to make sure you can have your say.

✓ Give you your own space to enable you to do things by yourself (as long as its safe for you to do so).

Unhelpful things grown-ups can do:

X Choose the solution they think is best, rather than listening to what you need.

X Make you feel like problems cannot be fixed.

X Interrupt you or not allow you to have your say.

X Talk to other grown-ups in your life about you in a way you are uncomfortable with.

X Make decisions that affect your care without telling you.

X Not allow you to do things by yourself (even when you know you can).

Is there anything else you would add to these lists?

_____

_____

One of the many cool things about my parents was that if I had a problem with the way they handled things, they were willing to listen and have a chat about what they could do differently. Some grown-ups were less willing though! If you're struggling to talk to the adults in your life about your needs (and believe me, this can still be hard even when you're a grown-up!), then here are some handy hints for getting the conversation started:

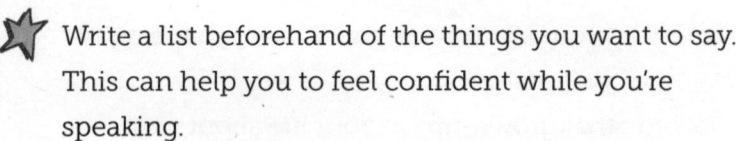 Write a list beforehand of the things you want to say. This can help you to feel confident while you're speaking.

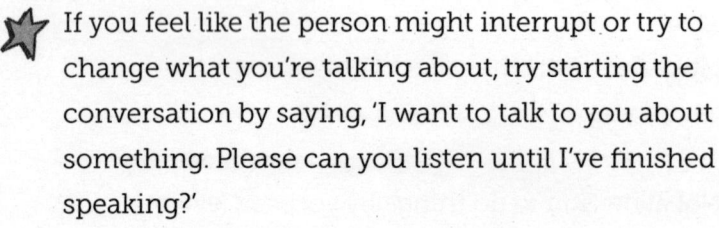 If you feel like the person might interrupt or try to change what you're talking about, try starting the conversation by saying, 'I want to talk to you about something. Please can you listen until I've finished speaking?'

 You don't have to have one big conversation – it could be a few smaller chats. If you feel like you forgot something or didn't say something in the way you wanted to, you can come back to it another time.

 If you don't feel comfortable talking face-to-face, you could write them a note or ask another adult you trust to start a conversation, with or without you.

My parents didn't have accessibility issues like I did, and never faced bullying or discrimination because of the way people thought about disability. But they saw what I went through because they were often with me when those things happened. They often felt sad or angry about the ableism or inaccessibility I experienced, and they fought for me to be treated fairly. Whether your parents or caregivers are disabled or non-disabled, it's important to remember that the challenges in your life aren't yours to face alone – your family or the people caring for you have a responsibility to advocate for you and your rights too.

Advocate: when someone advocates for something or someone, they support it publicly, talk to people in charge and try to improve things. For example, when our parents or carers advocate for us to have access to something that we've never had access to before, they might write letters or talk to teachers, doctors or people in charge of the things we need.

WHEN ADULTS DON'T GET IT

Some adults feel shy talking about disability, or ignore it completely and expect disabled kids to be able to do all the things non-disabled kids can do. That could be because the adult doesn't want to accept their kid is disabled, or because they feel uncomfortable talking about it, or even because they just don't understand the child's disability. This can put a lot of pressure on the child to know when to stand up for themselves or ask for what they need.

If you are reading this, then I'm guessing you have supportive adults who recognize your needs and the barriers that you face (that's probably how you ended up reading this book!).

But it's possible that you, or maybe someone you know, might have a family member that doesn't seem to recognize you or your disability. My friend Junior grew up with a parent who wasn't disabled when Junior was a kid, but became disabled later in life. They explained to me that it was only once their mum became disabled that she began to understand how much Junior had to struggle with.

> *My mum's disabilities came about when I was in my late teens, and it finally led to understanding. It made her see how much effort I was putting in to trying to mask every single day.*

While Junior says it was tough when they were young and their mum didn't really 'get it', they think their bumpy journey has helped them to find a path of self-acceptance.

> *It made me realize that I had to accept who I was and helped me to choose my path in life. I found ways to show people that I could do these amazing things too.*

If, like Junior, you have a family member or other adult in your life who doesn't seem to recognize your disability, then I want you to know this is not your fault and that you are not responsible for educating them about it. The best thing to do is to speak to another adult who you can trust about how you feel and what can be done, and not try to manage things all by yourself. You could try showing the other adult – or even the person who doesn't get it, if you feel comfortable to – this chapter, to help start the conversation.

Masking

Masking is something many disabled people do to hide our behaviour and symptoms and on occasions when we want to fit into an environment where we feel it isn't safe for us to be ourselves. All disabled people do this to some extent, but for many neurodivergent people, masking is often the only way they can manage certain situations. When people mask, they might be hiding pain they're experiencing, their emotions or stimming (movements or sounds neurodivergent people make repeatedly to help manage their emotions). Masking involves hiding our true selves, which takes a lot of effort and can be very tiring.

But there are actually two definitions to the word 'masking' – the second means wearing a mask. This is something many people need to do in public spaces in order to prevent getting sick. When coronavirus started spreading in 2020 (do you remember that?), lots of people wore masks to keep themselves and others safe, but now less people wear them. My friend Lorna explains why she continues to wear a mask in public:

As someone who became disabled through getting sick, I mask to protect what's left of my health. I also want to show care for my community, and for me masking tells other disabled people, 'you belong in this space, you deserve to be protected.'

WE ARE FAMILY!

Okay, so we've talked about having tricky conversations with family – now let's talk about the good times. Who are the people in your family who you feel like you can really be yourself and have fun with?

Apart from my parents, for me that was my brother and sister. They were among the first people in my life to accept and love me the way I was, and plus, because they were older than me, I thought they were really cool. My older sister was into make-up and girl bands, and one year for my birthday she bought me a poster of one of my favourite girl bands, All Saints. She even got one of the band members to sign it!

With my brother, I enjoyed play-fighting and climbing on his back. I loved having the freedom to have fun and mess about with my siblings.

Although they lived far away, and they couldn't share my experiences as a person with dwarfism, my brother and sister were really important to me as I was growing up as I could be 100 per cent myself around them, and I never needed to worry about what they thought about my disability.

Do you have siblings who are older or younger than you, or maybe a mix? Are they disabled too? Perhaps you have half-siblings like me, stepsiblings, or maybe cousins who you are close to. Or maybe you have a chosen family – people you aren't related to but who know you inside out and accept you completely. (We'll talk more about those awesome kinds of people in Chapter 5!) Which people in your life do you feel really loved and accepted by? **Have a go at writing them down.**

People who love and accept me just as I am . . .

ADOPTION

Are you adopted, or do you know anyone who is? My friend Ellie Simmonds is, and she has told me a bit about her experience for this book. You've probably heard Ellie's name before – she is a retired Paralympic swimmer (and gold medal winner!), TV personality and public speaker. She was also a contestant on *Strictly Come Dancing* in 2022. Ellie has inspired me for a long time – not because she's disabled, but because she's unafraid to try challenging things, and she also happens to be a really lovely person. Ellie has achondroplasia dwarfism and was adopted by average-height parents. This is her story:

I was fostered when I was two weeks old and adopted at six months. I can't remember that time, but I've always known I was adopted – there was never an announcement about it; it was just something I've always been aware of. I've always had a box with all my adoption information in it, and a dress and a few toys from my birth family and my foster family. My siblings – there's five of us – are all adopted too; it was something our parents have always been really open about.

> *I am the second person in my family to have dwarfism, as my older sister has it too. The social workers saw my parents already had another child with dwarfism when they placed me. Our parents are average height. As a family we are so accepting of disabilities* [one of Ellie's other siblings has learning disabilities] *and I've grown up around disabled people of different ages. It gives you a better outlook on life, a greater acceptance that we're all different.*

Maybe you have an adoptive family like Ellie's. If so, what do you love about your family? Do you have other adopted siblings, and are they disabled too?

Adopting a disabled child is an awesome thing to do, and we could do with more amazing parents like Ellie's in the world. Of course, there are sometimes tough bits to being a parent of disabled kids, like managing medical appointments and needing extra money for special equipment, and many people who are looking to adopt worry that they might struggle to look after a disabled child. But if society were a more inclusive place to raise disabled children, a lot of those worries simply wouldn't be an issue. And, as Ellie says, being part of a family with disabled kids is a really wonderful thing that gives you a more accepting perspective on life.

BECOMING A DISABLED PARENT LATER (IF YOU WANT TO!)

I knew from a really young age that I wanted to have children of my own, if I could. Perhaps you've thought about this too, or maybe it seems like WAY too far away to think about. There's no rush and it's totally cool to *not* want to have children when you're older, or to change your mind about it however many times you want!

I knew there was a good chance that if I had kids naturally, they would have dwarfism too, and I really liked the idea that we might share that. Achondroplasia dwarfism is genetic – which means it can be passed down from parent to child.

? **Gene (or genetic):** a part of a cell that is passed down from a birth parent to a child and which controls a characteristic of your brain and/or body. A genetic disability is one where the gene is passed down.

Not all disabilities are genetic, and some genetic disabilities are more likely to be passed down than others. It varies! Do you know whether your disability could be passed down to future kids, if you have them? How do you feel about that?

Whether you decide to have children or not in the future is completely up to you. You might have lots of children; want just one or two; or maybe you'd prefer a house full of cats or other furry friends. Perhaps you want to live life on the go when you're an adult and travel the world! It's your choice, and you definitely don't need to decide now.

If like me you do decide to have children, and you're likely to share your disability with your kids, then the brilliant thing is that your future kids will benefit from having an awesome disabled role model – that's YOU!

MY FAMILY TODAY

Now that I'm an adult, I have two children who both have the same disability as me. They also both *really* look like me! I love the way my family tree looks now. It feels complete.

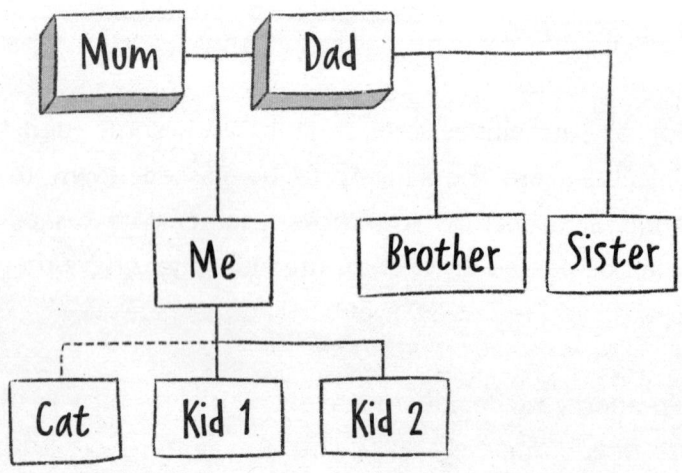

I think my kids' childhoods have – so far – been quite different to mine, and a big part of that is because they both have a sister who has dwarfism and a mum who has it too. As we heard from my friend Ivy, seeing your disability in the people who surround you and love you goes a long way to normalize and celebrate that part of your identity from the beginning. But just because I have dwarfism too doesn't mean I'm a perfect parent to my kids, and I *definitely* don't get things right all the time.

Sometimes us disabled parents might think our children's experiences are the same as ours, when actually there are lots of things that make them different. And sometimes we're not very good at remembering that our kids have their own unique personalities, feelings and emotions, and aren't just smaller versions of us.

I can be a bit overprotective of my kids (and now I understand why my parents were like this towards me!), because I don't want them to experience the same negative attitudes or inaccessibility that I did. But I also have to remind myself that the way they want to deal with those situations might be different to the way I would deal with them, and as their parent it's important to listen to them and put their feelings first. After all, it's not my life – it's theirs!

OVER TO YOU

In this chapter, we've talked about different kinds of families, how to speak to family about disability, the family members you can have fun with, and even future families. So it feels like now might be a good moment to reflect on what YOUR family is like, the things they do for you that make you feel supported – or things you'd like them to do more of.

How my family supports me:

_____

_____

_____

_____

What I'd like them to do more of:

_____

_____

_____

_____

If you feel able, it might be good to have a chat with some people in your family about what you've written down, or any of the other points in this chapter. That way they can continue learning about how they can be the best advocates for and supporters of you.

Whether your family gets it wrong or right or – like most of us – a bit of both, the adults who care for us at home aren't the only people we can go to for help and support. As I mentioned before, there are loads of other people we can chat to, including our friends and other grown-ups who are there to help us, like teachers and support staff at school. Which brings us nicely on to our next chapter...

But before we move on, here are some important reminders about family:

Lots of disabled kids have disabled parents or carers. Lots of disabled kids have non-disabled parents or carers. Some parent-carers are disabled in different ways to their children. Some parents aren't disabled when we are young, but become disabled later. **Families are all different, and that's cool!**

Your family doesn't have to be limited to just the people that you're related to. Your family could be just you and one other person, or more people. It could be made up of family members, friends or carers, or a mix of all three. You get to choose who you consider family.

 Grown-ups don't always get things right and there might be times when someone in your family isn't supporting you in the right way. And because ableism is everywhere in our society, **sometimes a family member might have an ableist viewpoint, probably without even realizing it**. It's okay to tell a family member when they're getting it wrong (you could use the tips in this chapter to have a chat with them about it) – or if you're not comfortable doing that, think about letting another trusted adult know so they can support you.

 You deserve a family that is fully accepting of who you are and your disabled self – one that celebrates you and advocates for you in ways you're comfortable with.

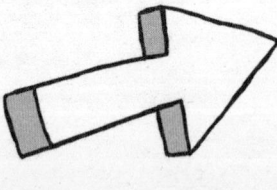

CHAPTER 3

Back to School

Oh my god. Something REALLY embarrassing just happened.

For the first time, I was invited to sit with the Year 6s in the canteen at lunch. It was amazing! I was so excited I couldn't sit still. And then, just as I was munching on my cheese-and-pickle brown bread sandwich, something awful happened.

I wet myself.

HELP! I tried to hide it by acting normally, then when someone noticed I quickly lied and said I'd sat in something wet . . . but I'm 1,000 per cent sure everyone knew the truth. If all of that wasn't embarrassing enough already, one of the LAs (lunchtime assistant – an adult who helps kids at lunchtime) noticed and pulled me by the arm out of the canteen.

I never want to go to school ever again!

This story sounds really embarrassing, doesn't it? Well, guess what – this actually happened to me. Luckily I survived to tell the tale, but at the time it felt like The Worst Thing That Ever Happened.

I was nine years old and over the moon to be invited to sit with a group of older girls. One of them was even Head Girl! But my proud moment quickly turned into a seriously awkward one.

The worst bit was that the LA made me feel as though wetting myself was somehow my fault. But I couldn't control it – it was just something that happened when I was excited or nervous, partly because of my disability. She made me feel ashamed and embarrassed, as though my body was broken.

If anyone has ever made you feel like this, then I want you to know that this is **absolutely not okay.** But you might find as you go through school (and through life) that adults often expect the same things from you as they would from a non-disabled child. And then when you can't do those things or need longer to do them, they might assume you're not trying hard enough instead of realizing you need to do things differently. This can be really tough to deal with.

> But I want you to know that YOU are not the problem – it's other people's attitudes that need to change.

In this chapter we're going to go back to school (well, 'back' for me at least) and talk about how you can deal with some of these (totally rubbish) attitudes and expectations so you can just get on with the important stuff, like figuring out how to spell rude words on your calculator.

Anyway, talking about things that are totally rubbish (at least, as far as I'm concerned), our next section is all about . . .

P.E., A.K.A. SPORTS, A.K.A. RUNNING, A.K.A. NO WAY, NO THANKS, GOODBYE!

I used to find P.E. really hard. Plenty of kids – including disabled kids – love P.E., but I was very shy and not very good at sports. I hated running because I used to fall over a lot and often hit my head, then everyone would rush over and make a HUGE deal out of it, when all I wanted was to pretend nothing had happened. Plus, I was so much

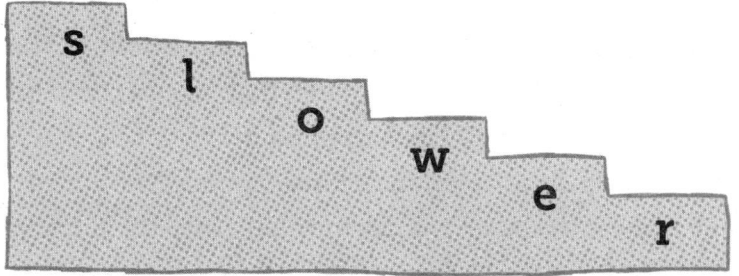

than everyone else, even when I tried my best. So my solution was that I just didn't run at all. Sometimes I pretended to feel unwell so I could skip P.E. lessons altogether (please don't do this – it didn't help, and it just gave me more anxiety for the next lesson!). In the end, my school agreed that I didn't have to do P.E. any more because it was too hard for me, so I sat at the side doing my homework instead.

When I think about it now, it's clear that I needed support that I just wasn't getting. Rather than telling me P.E. was too hard for me, a better solution would have been for the school to provide me with adaptations to allow me to join in.

Adaptation: a change that needs to be made to a piece of equipment or an activity so that it is accessible for you.

For example, I had a chair with a footrest both in the classroom and the school canteen that I could climb on and off easily and which supported my back so it didn't hurt. That's an adaptation. Before I stopped doing P.E., my teacher would let me start further down the track in running races, so I had a chance of not always coming last! That's an adaptation too.

At school I often dreaded P.E., but if I'd been given the right adaptations, I think I could have enjoyed it so much more. I liked playing games and moving my body; I just didn't like that it always felt like a competition I would never win. Maybe if school had also let us enjoy sport sometimes just for the fun of it – without there needing to be winners and losers – I wouldn't have felt such pressure.

How do you feel about P.E.? Is there a particular sport you really enjoy that you just don't have the right support to do fully at school? When I had swimming lessons with my class, we started off in the big pool, where they could all stand up, but I couldn't! It was so much harder for me to complete the lesson, but it could've easily been made accessible if the lesson had been adapted so I could swim in the shallow pool.

Some other examples of adaptations that schools can put in place to support disabled pupils are:

⭐ providing adapted equipment, such as sports wheelchairs or pedal exercisers.

⭐ adapting team sports to allow disabled students to take part – for example, using a smaller-sized playing field and having students walk or wheel instead of run.

⭐ using lowered baskets or nets, bigger goals or targets.

⭐ giving pupils extra time for competitive games or letting them compete from a closer range if they need it.

⭐ having a clearly marked quiet space where students can take breaks from noisy activities, and another area where students can take movement breaks and use stress balls or fidget toys.

removing individual competition and focusing on group games and sports. When activities involve teamwork, it helps us build the super-important skills of both working together to achieve something and discovering and using everyone's individual strengths.

The good news is that many primary schools in the UK now offer lots more ways for kids to exercise, like yoga and dance, and some schools even offer swimming lessons that are adapted for different levels. And there's a lot more teamwork than there used to be. But if you're not getting the support you need in P.E. or you're feeling worried about it, then it's really important to speak to a trusted adult who can let your school know about any adaptations you may need.

You deserve to enjoy moving your body just as much as anyone else!

The Paralympics

I should add here that not every disabled person hates P.E., or is bad at sports – in fact, loads of disabled people love sports and many are really good at different games. Giving disabled people the opportunity to play with or compete against other disabled people makes sports fairer for us, and it also makes it way more fun and exciting. Have you heard of the Paralympics? It's a big international sporting event that happens every four years in which disabled people from all over the world take part in things like swimming, javelin and basketball competitions. It's a great celebration of all the amazing disabled sporting talent in the world.

OTHER CHALLENGES AT SCHOOL

Here's Ellie from → Chapter 2!

Maybe P.E. is a breeze for you, or maybe you face some other barriers in school that aren't related to sports and exercise. My biggest challenge was P.E., but I had others too. Have you had difficulties similar to any of the ones that follow, or maybe something else entirely?

Noisy lunchroom

So many people in one space, loud conversations, the scraping and clattering of chairs, forks and plates, kids running around everywhere ... It's a lot for the senses to handle! The chaos of the canteen can be overwhelming at times. I used to feel anxious about where I would sit and who with, plus I needed help to carry my tray and cut up my food.

The noisiness of lunch and breaktimes can be particularly tricky for neurodivergent kids. If you're struggling with noisy, busy spaces, it's helpful to know that your school has a responsibility to make adaptations for you. That could include having a quiet space away from the hustle and bustle to eat in and talk to your friends, or maybe being let out for playtime a bit earlier than some of the other kids.

Inaccessible playground

Are you able to fully move around your playground and use all the equipment? If your playground is inaccessible for you, it might be worth telling your adult about it and holding a meeting with the school to see how they can adapt things for you. Most schools have a caretaker, and one of their jobs is to manage all the equipment, so it's worth finding out what's possible. Sometimes schools raise extra funds from their PTA and local businesses – maybe some of this money could be used for some play equipment that's accessible for you?

Handwriting

What's your handwriting like? Do you find it easy or difficult writing in a way that is clear for others to read? Perhaps you use special pens, a laptop or something else to help you?

I'm left-handed and have short, wide fingers, so I used to find it tricky to get my letters to look like everyone else's. One of my teachers in secondary school used to make me feel bad for not having perfect handwriting. It shouldn't have mattered because you could still read my writing just fine. I wish I could've told that teacher that by the time I'd be an adult I'd be typing most things I want to write anyway! But more to the point, my teacher could have just accepted that everyone writes differently, and that **however I write is good enough**.

Extra time

Do you find it hard to keep up, and need more time to think, prepare or write your work? I was slower than other pupils at writing due to my small fingers, so I needed extra time for tests. Luckily teachers got on board quickly and let me have it. It often cut into my break times though, meaning I got less time outside with everyone else, which was a bit annoying!

The barriers you face in education might be similar or different to the ones I've listed here. What lessons or aspects of school life feel tricky for you? Which bits make it easier for you to navigate those things?

FIXING THE SYSTEM

If certain parts of your education are inaccessible to you, it's not because you're disabled – it's because your access needs haven't been met by your school. Why does this happen though?

> **?**
>
> **Access needs:** the requirements you have in order to be able to access something in the same way as everyone else –for example, subtitles, dim lighting, or a quiet space away from the noise.

Well, there are lots of different factors that work together to create barriers for us in education, as well as in other areas of our lives. In a school setting, this might look like:

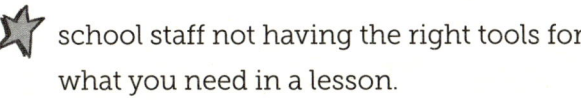 school staff not having the right tools for what you need in a lesson.

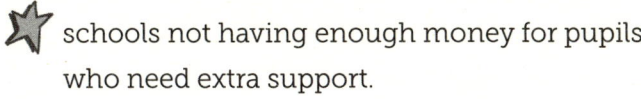 staff not having the right attitudes, or not receiving the right training, to help you.

 schools not having enough money for pupils who need extra support.

 the pressures school staff are under to support all kids at all times – it can be a very stressful job!

academic achievements and opportunities being inaccessible to some pupils. (We can't all get an A in Maths, and that's okay.)

sports-based achievements and opportunities being inaccessible to some pupils. (We can't all be the fittest, fastest or strongest, and that's okay too.)

the school's physical environment being unsuitable for your needs, and no money or resources being available to fix it.

These different factors come together to create a system that is inaccessible – and it's that system that needs fixing, not the disabled pupils. This goes beyond just your school environment; it's also to do with how much money the school receives from the government, and *that* is partly to do with how much the government sees accessibility as something that's super important . . . I know – complicated, right?!

The important thing you should remember is that something being inaccessible to you is never ever your fault. Having a brain and/or body that works differently to other people's doesn't mean that you are not as valuable or awesome as everyone else. And needing things to be done differently for you shouldn't mean you don't get to do them.

The system is what needs to change – not you!

The good news is that schools are (mostly) a lot better at supporting disabled kids now than they were when I was your age. There's even a law (the Equality Act 2010) that says schools must do everything they can to make sure children who are disabled and/or who have special educational needs (SEN) get the support they need. This law also says schools cannot discriminate against disabled pupils, which means they have to make the school setting accessible and safe for them. That includes you!

Special schools

While all schools have a responsibility to support their disabled students, sometimes a mainstream school (that is, an average primary or secondary school) won't be able to provide the level of support that's needed for a particular child. This is where special schools (sometimes called specialist schools or settings) come in. Special schools are there to support disabled children who require a higher level of support than can be given at a mainstream school. They tend to be smaller, and usually – but not always – the pupils are all disabled. Lots of disabled children benefit from attending special schools, while many also benefit from attending a mainstream school. Neither is better than the other; it just depends on what works best for each kid. What kind of school do you go to?

You are just as **valuable** and **awesome** as everyone else, no matter how your brain and body works.

SUPPORT AT SCHOOL

If you need extra help at school and you're not getting it, you and your parent or carer need to find out which member of staff is best to talk to. And then your adult can put their office phone number on speed dial!

Someone whose job it is to help you get the support you need is a SENCO. All schools in the UK have a SENCO, and their job is to organize any extra support kids need to access education. They also make sure all the other teachers and adults working at the school know how to help too. Remember, it is the responsibility of the people running the school to make the adaptations necessary so that your education is as accessible as possible for you. So whatever you need – don't be afraid to ask.

? **SENCO:** someone whose job it is to support kids who have special educational needs to access education. This support is available for children between the ages of five and fifteen in England and Wales (the rules are slightly different in other parts of the UK).

Some of the things a SENCO does are:

★ tell your parents or carer about any needs you have that they might not be aware of.

★ support you in finding and trying out the right support, equipment and adaptations you need at school.

★ talk to your healthcare providers (e.g. doctors) about your changing needs.

If there's just no way you can do a lesson or activity – even once it's been adapted – that's okay too! All of us have things that we are good at, things we're not so good at and things that we may not be able to do at all. It's important that you or your grown-ups let the school know if there's a lesson or activity that won't be possible for you to take part in so that they can provide you with an alternative.

KNOWING WHO TO ASK FOR HELP

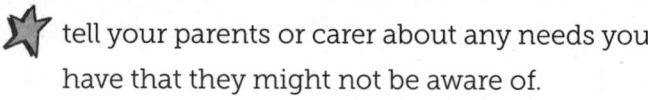

Your grown-ups are there to advocate for you, and you don't need to handle all of this school stuff by yourself.

But it's also important that you feel comfortable speaking to school staff about the support you need, especially when things come up during the school day and your grown-ups aren't there to help you.

Remember in the last chapter when we talked about helpful and unhelpful things grown-ups can do? Well, this also applies to the staff who are there to support you at school. Which members of staff do you feel most comfortable talking to?

I had a couple of teachers in Reception and Year 5 who really got it. They were two very different people, but the one thing they had in common was they both had empathy. They wanted to understand and to support me. Their empathy towards me meant I felt totally safe and able to be myself.

? **Empathy:** when you feel the same things someone else is feeling by imagining what it would be like to be in that person's situation – for example, when you feel sad because your friend has had a bad day.

Who is or are your helpful grown-up(s) at school? It might be your SENCO, lunchtime or office staff, or your favourite teacher. Write down a list of people you can go to if you need support – this can be a useful first step towards voicing your needs. And remember, you can always speak to your adults at home too and ask them to advocate on your behalf.

Helpful adults at school:

☆ _____

☆ _____

☆ _____

☆ _____

☆ _____

This next bit is up to you. If you're struggling in any of your lessons because they're not adapted to your needs, you've got to

SPEAK UP!

KNOWING *WHEN* TO ASK FOR HELP

One other important thing to remember is that our support needs change all the time. Sometimes we need more or less help. I needed someone to help me in the toilets up until about Year 4, but after that I managed to go by myself, so I let the school staff know. And I didn't need extra writing time until we started to write longer texts in around Year 5.

So while it's important to know WHO to ask for help, it's also important to know WHEN to ask for help. And because everyone's needs are different, it's super important to write a list of the barriers you face. For example:

I can't hold a pen the same way as others.

I can't hear my teacher when it's noisy.

I can't keep up with other kids in P.E.

. . . and so on. That way, when you meet the person helping you, you can work together to figure out what support you need.

You belong in your class (and in the playground too) and you deserve the same education as anyone else – the boring bits, the hard bits, the easy bits and the fun bits!

We've talked about what you can do, so now it's down to you:

If you feel like you need more support at school, **talk to an adult you can trust**, like your parent, carer, teacher, SENCO or the person whose job it is to support pupils at your school.

If you think it would be a good idea, ask your trusted parent or carer to **organize a meeting at the school** to discuss what you need.

You know your body and your brain better than anyone – don't be afraid to tell people exactly what changes you think would work for you, whether that's extra writing time, extra time in P.E., someone to help you in the toilets or something else. **You deserve to participate if you want to and to be given a fair chance in every lesson or activity**.

 If the changes that are made for you aren't quite right or your needs change after a while, **speak up** and let a grown-up know.

If something is inaccessible to you, and you really want to be able to do it, **try not to lose faith**. Look for opportunities to try again later. You might find new ways of doing things, or the school might be able to help even if they couldn't before.

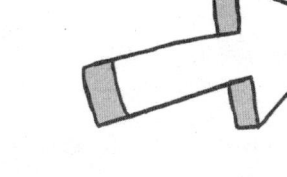

CHAPTER 4

BIG and SCARY School

Maybe you're in secondary school already, or you're about to start, or you've still got a couple more years to go. How do you feel about it?

Even though I may seem REALLY OLD to you, I can still remember feeling *very* scared on my first day of secondary school. I remember thinking how *big* everyone was, and I felt like a tiny dot. Would anyone even notice me? I wondered. Or would they treat me like I was invisible?

Most kids can relate to feeling a bit nervous on their first day of secondary school. But if you're disabled, there's a load of other stuff to think about – such as:

I didn't have to worry about some of this stuff, because the school I went to was actually tiny – so tiny in fact, that it was in a building in my headmistress's garden! Weird, right? I always wondered whether one day we'd see her watering her flowers in her dressing gown and slippers. She had lots of cats and kittens who would sometimes escape from her house and run around in our classrooms!

My secondary school was mostly accessible for me. As the building was quite small, we had all our lessons in the same room; I always used the same toilet; and the small class size meant that I wasn't badly bullied. (Let's face it, it's quite hard to get away with being horrible when there's only six of you in the class!) I still struggled with a lot of things though – like making friends, holding my pen in a way that didn't make my fingers ache, and That Age When Everyone Suddenly Becomes Obsessed With Snogging.

So my secondary-school experience was pretty unique, and it was probably very different to yours, especially if you go to a very BIG school. A lot of the issues are similar though. My friend Joy, who is blind, went to a massive secondary school – she told me a bit about how that went for her.

 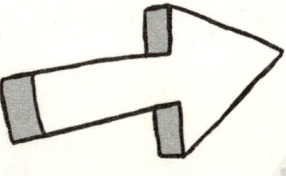

Even though it was difficult at first, I'm glad my mum made the decision to send me to a mainstream school. Navigating secondary school was hard because I was still learning to accept my disability myself. I didn't accept it for years – I was embarrassed to use a cane while walking to the bus stop or in school, because I didn't want to be seen as different. It wasn't until I got to sixteen or seventeen that I realized that I needed to accept my disability if I wanted other people to. I feel like secondary school shaped me and gave me a thicker skin.

It can be really hard to deal with the pressure to 'fit in' that comes at this age, particularly as a disabled kid. Like Joy, I often didn't want to show others that I needed extra help, or that I did things differently to them. Have you ever felt like that? If you have, you're not the only one. And as Joy learned, accepting yourself is the first step towards feeling accepted by others.

There might be things in what Joy and I have shared that are similar to your experiences, and there might be things that are different. There are lots of things I learned along the way through secondary school that will almost definitely be helpful to you too. Think of me as your super-cool older sibling who also happens to be disabled too. Maybe I've got spiky hair and a nose piercing and awesome tattoos and perfectly-winged eyeliner . . . okay, I'm getting carried away. Here are my . . .

TOP TIPS FOR STARTING SECONDARY SCHOOL

Tip 1 Ask for what you need

It's super important that you feel accepted and supported in your new school from the beginning. It's normal to feel nervous, and you'll probably think of a million questions, like:

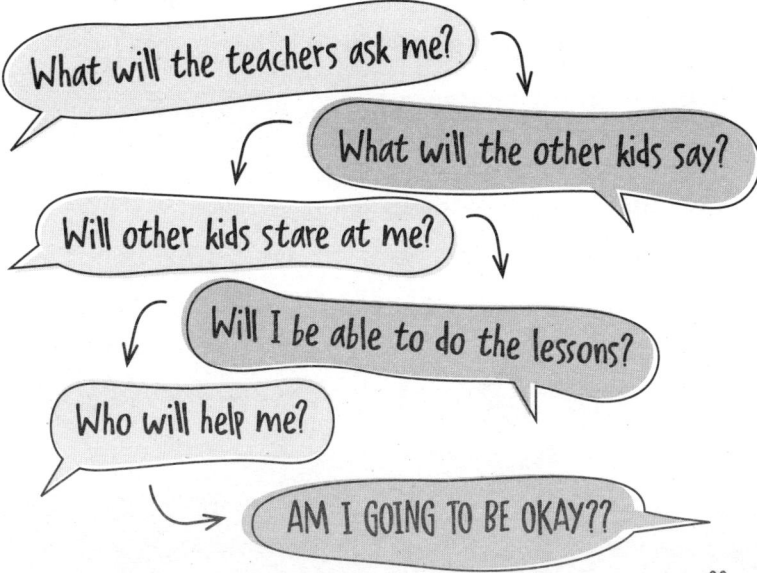

What will the teachers ask me?

What will the other kids say?

Will other kids stare at me?

Will I be able to do the lessons?

Who will help me?

AM I GOING TO BE OKAY??

The best way to calm these worries is to be prepared and ask for what you need in advance as much as possible. Get your parent or responsible adult to organize meetings with your form tutor, the person in charge of pastoral support (or student wellbeing), the SENCO and the head teacher before term starts. In some cases, depending on your needs, a representative from your local council might be there too. If you decide to be in the meeting, don't be afraid to ask as many questions as you want! If you don't want to be there, let your adult know what you'd like them to say or ask.

The most important question that your adult can ask is this:

What will your school do to make sure my child (that's YOU!) feels supported and welcome in every class?

And here are some more detailed questions that you or your adult might want to ask (some might not apply to you):

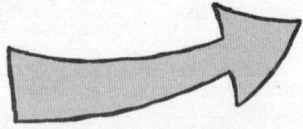

 Can I have a map showing where my classrooms are?

 Will someone (like a one-to-one assistant) always be available to help me? What kind of things will they help me with?

 Is it possible to change my timetable so my classrooms are closer together, or so I can have a break after P.E.?

 Can I have extra time to do reading/ writing/practical assignments if I need it?

 Where can I leave my wheelchair safely while I'm not using it?

 I will need special equipment in class. How will you make sure it's always available for me to use?

 Who will be my form tutor? What support can they give me?

⭐ What is P.E. like? Is it possible to adapt the lessons so I can still do them?

⭐ What are break times like? How do you support disabled kids at break time?

⭐ Are there quiet areas where I can do my work, eat and spend break times? Can I bring a friend to sit with me during those times?

⭐ What do I do if I need the toilet in the middle of class? Who will help me in the toilets if I need it?

⭐ If my class goes on a school trip, can I bring an adult with me for support?

⭐ What do you do when one of the pupils comes to you and says they're being bullied or teased by other kids?

⭐ If I need help in an emergency, who do I speak to?

Of course, you might have different questions to those ones, so **feel free to add them here**.

_____

_____

_____

_____

Depending on your access needs, your local area may have government-funded buses and taxis available to take you to and from school when you reach secondary school. If this is something you think you will need, ask your adult to investigate this with your local authority as soon as you know which school you're going to, as it can take a while to organize.

Tip 2 Make a list of things you need

One thing that feels a bit terrifying about secondary school is just how much STUFF you're told you need. Before you start, your school will give you a list of things to buy – but you might not actually need all the things on the list. It's a great idea to go through the list with your adult and put all the items into two categories:

1. Things I **definitely** need, and

2. Things I **might** need.

For all the things you put in the second category, you might want to wait until school starts to decide whether you really need to buy them or not. Lots of people will be doing the same thing, so you won't be the only one. And you won't need everything every day either. When you have your timetable, you can figure out when you need your P.E. kit, history books, etc, and just bring them in on those days. It might be helpful to make a list of the stuff you'll need every day, and the stuff you'll only need on certain days.

Accessible Fonts

Do you have access to a kindle or a tablet you can read books on? Those are brilliant for anyone who needs help with reading. These devices can help with adjusting the text size and colour contrast, converting text to speech – plus, they mean you have fewer heavy books to lug about! SENCOs can often help with access to these and any other technology you might find useful.

As I was slower at writing and found it hard to keep up in secondary school, I was given a dictaphone (an old-fashioned recording device) to record important things my teacher said. I still have it in a box somewhere! Nowadays you can do that on your mobile phone or laptop.

Tip 3 Only tell people the stuff you want to share

New school, new you! This is an opportunity for you to decide how much you want people to know about your disability. It's hard enough starting a new school and meeting a bunch of new faces, but it can be even harder when you're a disabled kid and everyone *immediately* has loads of questions about why you are the way you are. Some disabled kids find it helps to talk to their teachers and classmates about their disability early on, so they can answer any questions they might have in one big conversation and just get it all out the way.

Other disabled kids (like me when I was a kid) can't think of *anything worse*! I hated when people spoke about my disability in class or asked me questions (unless they were my mates – that was different). It felt like it was none of their business! What was also annoying was that I often felt like I had to answer people, especially teachers ... and that didn't always make me feel very good. I wasn't at school to teach people about myself; I was there to *learn*.

However you feel, remember, **you don't have to explain anything to anyone if you don't want to**. But there will probably be some questions at some point, so it might be a good idea to have a think about how you're going to tackle those questions and comments from other kids and teachers. Some possible responses could be:

Yes, I have ————————
Some other facts about me are that my favourite colour is baby blue and I LOVE fantasy football/ Beyoncé/[insert other thing you love here]!
How about you?

I don't want to answer that question. Can we talk about something else?

I'm not comfortable sharing that.

> You get to decide what other people need to know about you, so say whatever feels best for you.

I wish that more people had told me when I was your age that it's perfectly okay to say, 'I don't want to talk about that.' After all, there are plenty more interesting and fun conversations you could be having instead!

Tip 4 Remember, you are exactly where you belong

Even though sometimes it can feel like the world wasn't built for you, remember that you deserve the same school experience as everyone else. **You deserve to be there.**

Your body and/or your brain might work differently to a lot of people's, but your needs are just as important as theirs. Education should be available to you and accessible for you. And you should be able to enjoy it! (Okay, okay – most of it. My Year 8 project on fossilization wasn't what I called fun . . .)

As we've already talked about, sadly there are certain parts of school – and society in general – that are inaccessible to lots of people. But because so much is accessible to the majority of people, it can feel like nobody cares about the ones who get left behind.

I promise you there are people who genuinely care and are working to make the world a more accessible place for everyone. We can do our part by speaking out and directly telling people what we need, even when it's scary.

OVER TO YOU

What are some of the things you find inaccessible in the school you're in right now?

☆ _____

☆ _____

☆ _____

☆ _____

☆ _____

How could each of those things be changed to be made more accessible for you?

☆ _____

☆ _____

☆ _____

☆ _____

☆ _____

Here are some ideas for starting a conversation with teachers and school staff about the examples you wrote down above:

⭐ Can I talk to you about what I need in class?

⭐ I'm struggling to keep up. Could we chat about it?

⭐ My bag is really heavy. Is there someone who can help me carry it to class?

⭐ I am really tired. Is there somewhere I can rest in my free period?

⭐ I am finding things hard but I'm not sure what I need. Can you help me work it out?

Tip 5 You don't need to have it all figured out

This chapter might feel a bit overwhelming. Figuring out what your needs are can be overwhelming. Talking about your needs can be overwhelming. Asking for what you need can be overwhelming. And sometimes we don't even know what we need until we're actually there, in the classroom, needing whatever it is that we need. I just want to quickly say: **all of that is normal.**

There have been so many times when I haven't known I needed support, or asked for the wrong thing, or asked for something and then not needed it after all! Be kind to yourself – no matter how prepared you are, you're not going to be able to plan everything perfectly. It's just good to try and think about these things ahead of time so you're at least aware of any potentially sticky situations – and what to do if you find yourself in one.

P.S. – There's no such thing as a perfect disabled person who always knows what they need and how to get it. I'm certainly not perfect at that, and I'll bet you're not either. And that's okay!

Tip 6 Remember, you are not alone

Most people find secondary school one of the hardest times of their lives. Yep, even the most popular girl in class has problems. Our bodies are changing (more on that in Chapter 7); emotions are all over the place; you have to take your lessons seriously; everyone suddenly cares about how they look; and – what – we're getting spots and *smelly armpits* now as well? It's a lot!

When you're disabled, you've got all of the above to deal with and more. But if you think you're struggling alone, maybe it will help to remember that everyone has hard stuff going on. Connecting with other kids and supporting each other through the tough bits is really important.

It's so essential that we are able to find school friends that love and support and accept us exactly how we are. People who will help you through difficult times and make you feel less alone. With that said, let's move on to the next chapter . . .

We all need help sometimes – this is totally normal and you should **never, ever** be made to feel embarrassed to ask for it.

But before we exit the school gates, here are some reminders:

 Okay, so maybe Iniyah can run the fastest and Maisie is great at spelling and Jack has the neatest handwriting. That's all great for them – but you're awesome too. Your worth does not depend on whether you can run fast, have the neatest handwriting, or can spell difficult words. **Your worth depends on you being a kind, fun person** – which you already are.

 You deserve a **brilliant, interesting, fun, informative** and **accessible** experience at secondary school, just **like everyone else**.

 You should never be made to feel afraid of the place you learn in, or the other people in it. If you do – speak up to someone you can trust.

 Planning ahead and talking to adults can help relieve some of the pressure of those unknown things about your new school. But **there will probably be things you only figure out once you've started**. Remember to ask whoever is responsible for supporting you in your new school for help if you need it.

We all need help sometimes – this is totally normal and you should **never, ever feel embarrassed** to ask for it, or like you are causing a problem by needing it. You deserve support with the things you find tricky, and it's okay if you find things trickier than other people.

CHAPTER 5

Forever Friends

Right, now we're out of the school gates, we're going to talk about something much more fun – FRIENDS. If you're anything like me, you probably spend way more time thinking about your friendships than your schoolwork. (I mean, fractions aren't exactly hilarious ...)

$$\frac{25}{4} =$$

Do you find it easy to make new friends? Perhaps you'd really like to make some more disabled friends, but you're not sure where to start.

In this chapter, we're going to talk about different ways to form friendships and connect with other disabled kids, and we'll also look at relationships with non-disabled friends and how you can support them just as much as they can support you. And (although I wish we didn't have to), we'll also be sharing some tips for dealing with bullies and fake friends.

But first, let's start with one of the best bits about making friends as a disabled person ...

FINDING YOUR COMMUNITY

Your community are the people who love and understand you, who know what you're going through and can support you through your experiences – the good and bad.

Having disabled community is important because you can meet people who are going through similar things to you – people who 'get it' and can look out for each other.

My disabled friends were such a big part of my life when I was young, and they remain very important to me now.

It also helped when I was young to know disabled adults, because they showed me just by living their lives that I would be okay. Now I'm an adult, I have lots of disabled friends who have all different kinds of disabilities. There's a lot of things that people in the disabled community experience differently, but there's loads we have in common too. My disabled friends are the most welcoming and accepting bunch of people I've ever met!

Do you have any disabled friends? What do you love about those friendships? If you don't have any and would like to make some, or maybe you have some already but would like a few more, you could ask an adult to help you find a group or network for people who share your disability. Most areas of the UK have some kind of network you can join locally – such as a social group, sports club or swimming group – that's just for disabled people or kids. It might also be good for your parents or carers to meet other adults who care for disabled children, so they can get support too.

When I was younger, my parents took me to a dwarfism convention so we could meet people that looked like me. Yeah, I know 'convention' sounds kinda boring, but these ones are actually really cool. Dwarfism conventions are events where lots of people who have dwarfism (and their families) spend time together, talk about issues we face in our community, make friends and have SO MUCH FUN!

The conventions happen once a year over one weekend and are held in a really nice hotel. Usually there's some fun activities organized for the kids – you can swim in the hotel pool, dress up all fancy for a posh dinner and play bingo. So going to these conventions, not only did I get to meet other kids who had dwarfism, but we all got to stay in the same hotel and do cool stuff together too! I went from not seeing anybody that looked like me every single day to being in a place FULL of people that looked like me – and where people who were average height, like my parents, were the odd ones out! **It was awesome**.

Now I take my own kids to those same dwarfism conventions and I get to watch them having fun making new friends. It's very cool!

Rico, aged nine, also enjoys going to dwarfism conventions. Like me, he has achondroplasia dwarfism and the rest of his family are average height. I asked him what the conventions mean to him:

> *When I go to those events, I feel like I'm not the only one with dwarfism. I feel really happy because I can see people who have dwarfism like me, and it's good to meet up and socialize. I like making new friends.*

Outside of big conventions, Rico also goes to smaller local meet-ups with his family and sports events too.

> *It's nice to compete with people my size! When I do competitions at school, I'm the only one with dwarfism so there's loads of other people who are faster and taller than me. If I'm competing with other people with dwarfism, it's easier.*

Rico and I are both lucky enough to be part of inclusive spaces where we can just be ourselves. Perhaps you could ask your grown-ups to check whether there are similar events or spaces in your local area that cater to your disability? Nowadays there are loads more activities and community groups on offer for disabled kids compared to when I was growing up – from football teams to arts and crafts clubs, and dance companies. Which brings us to our next section...

SPECIAL INTERESTS

These are the things we love doing, no matter whether we are any good at them or not. Things that make us feel excited and alive and free.

When I was a kid, those things were:

⭐ **painting and drawing** – usually pictures of pop stars, clothes and food I really loved!

⭐ **listening to music and making up my own songs.** (I still remember the lyrics to a song I wrote when I was about eleven!)

⭐ **swimming** – I'm part of a disabled swimming group, which is local to me, and I love it! Through that I've made many other disabled friends.

⭐ **playing video games** (especially fantasy games like *The Sims*, which was a game a lot of kids played when I was young, where you could build cities and houses for your characters to live in).

Maybe you enjoy some of these things too, or something else? When I was doing my favourite hobbies, I felt like I could just be me. I wasn't thinking about my disability or how other people saw me; I could just enjoy creating things and moving my body in the ways that suited me best. What are some of the things you like doing that make you feel like this? Are there any groups local to you, like my swimming club, that you can join so you can meet others who enjoy the same things as you?

Things I love doing:

Do you like doing your hobbies alone or with other people? Some people prefer doing things on their own and that's totally okay, but others might enjoy some company.

Maybe you love coming up with dance routines and you'd like to find some friends to boogie with. Or perhaps you're a brilliant chess player and you're looking for people to play against. Whatever it is you love doing, sharing your passion with others is a fantastic way of making friends, as you'll already have something in common. Find out what clubs and activities are on offer at your school or ask your grown-up if they can help you research local clubs in your area. It could be a group specifically for disabled kids or one that's open to everyone – either way, connecting over a hobby is a brilliant way to meet new people.

MEETING FRIENDS ONLINE

The other great thing about hobbies and special interests is that often they can be shared and enjoyed with other people, even when you're not in the same room! Whether you love gaming, football, music or something completely different, the internet can be a great place to connect with people who share your interests.

It's also easy to find other kids who share your disability online. There are Facebook groups, forums and Whatsapp groups for parents of kids with different disabilities, so if you want to, ask your adult to find one for your disability where you live. Once they have connected with other parents or carers, you could ask if their kid wants to chat. It's important to do this safely and make sure both your adults and theirs agree before you start to talk. When I was your age, I wrote letters to my disabled friends – but now you can also video call or play games online together. The possibilities are endless!

The internet is a fantastic tool for meeting people and making friends but it's also really important that you protect yourself and your personal information online. You wouldn't give a stranger your personal details in the real world, and the same goes for the online world. With that in mind, here are my...

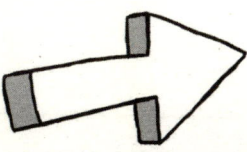

TOP TIPS FOR STAYING SAFE ONLINE:

Top tip 1 Protect your identity

Don't give out your address, phone number or anything else that identifies you to people you don't know.

Top tip 2 Protect your data

If you want to play a game or use a website that asks you to register before you access it, and the form asks for personal information such as your address and phone number, check with your adult first.

Top tip 3 It's okay to not respond

If someone tries to chat with you while you're playing a game online together, and you don't know them, you don't have to respond. If they say inappropriate things or things that make you feel uncomfortable, block them if you can or ask an adult to help.

Top tip 4 Talk to your grown-ups

If you'd like to arrange to meet an online friend, talk to your adult about it first. Never meet up with people you don't know without checking with an adult.

Top tip 5 Know your limits

Sometimes when we spend a lot of time staring at a screen, it can affect our moods negatively, and we can find it difficult to switch off. Make sure to limit your screentime so that you have enough time to enjoy the world around you too.

Right, now that's out of the way – go explore and have fun!

Whether you're interested in watching football and sending reactions to each other after every foul and penalty, writing a song with a mate, playing *Minecraft*, or finding the second-biggest Olivia Rodrigo fan, the internet is your oyster. (Or if you want to be old-school like me and write your friends letters and postcards instead, that's totally cool too 😄.)

REAL FRIENDS SUPPORT ONE ANOTHER!

Now that we've talked about some of the ways we can make new friends, we're going to speak about how your friends can be the best supporters of YOU – and how you can support them too.

I hope that you have a supportive disabled community around you (and if you don't, hopefully some of the tips so far have given you a good place to start), but it's likely that many of your friends will be non-disabled, particularly if you go to a mainstream school.

But sometimes non-disabled kids (just like some non-disabled adults!) can be **just-a-little-bit-clueless** about how to support their disabled friends – even when they genuinely just want to be your mate. That could be because their parents have never talked to them about disability, or maybe they've seen things on TV or in books that have shown disability in a negative way – or they've just not seen disability represented that much in the first place. This isn't really their fault and it's all to do with how society treats disability.

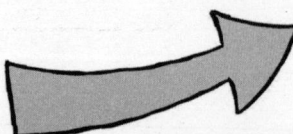

So if your friends get things wrong from time to time – for example, forgetting that you might not be able to do certain things or even trying to help you *too much* – try to be patient with them and find ways to let them know how they can better support you. It can be a bit scary at times, but putting your trust in others and believing that they want the best for you is important for building strong friendships.

Ultimately only you know how you'd like your friends to help you out – your mates aren't mind readers! If they're true friends then they won't mind lending a hand when they can, and they certainly shouldn't make you feel bad for asking. It can be scary sometimes to ask for help when you need it, but the worst that anyone can say back is 'no, sorry'. Saying no doesn't mean the person isn't your friend anymore; it just means they can't help you at that time. And remember this works both ways too – you don't always have to say yes to your friends, and it's okay to say no if you're too tired or aren't able to do what they've asked. This is called having good boundaries.

Boundaries: the limits and rules we set ourselves that enable us to say 'no' to things that we don't want to – or can't – do.

For most things in life we *all* need a bit of help. And that's normal and okay! In fact, it's kinda sorta how the world works. Disabled people often need a little more help because we live in a world that isn't made for us, and people might not always understand our needs. But non-disabled people also need help with things sometimes too.

You help other people, all the time – whether you know it or not! Have a think about the things you're really good at. How do you use your talents to help others, and how could you use them if you don't already?

I have always been good at writing and organizing information, so now I help my friends by giving them advice on their writing or helping them fill in forms. I'm also pretty good at cooking tasty meals! Some of the things my friends help me with include taking me somewhere in their car, passing me things I can't reach and carrying heavy things for me.

What things would you like other kids to help you with sometimes? Make a list here ...

Things I want or need help from
my friends with sometimes:

☆ _____

☆ _____

☆ _____

Things I can help my friends
with sometimes:

☆ _____

☆ _____

☆ _____

Real friendship is all about
supporting one another – it's
a two-way street!

You deserve to have friends who make you feel
supported, accepted and loved, and who feel supported,
accepted and loved by you too.

To me, real friends are people who:

- celebrate who you are.

- support you when you're feeling down.

- encourage you when you're feeling worried.

- enjoy spending time with you and make you feel happier when you're around them.

- make you feel safe and comfortable to be yourself.

- make plans with you and – as much as they can – stick to them.

- are super fun!

- never make fun of you or leave you out on purpose.

- help you out sometimes – and ask you for help sometimes too.

Is there anything else you would add to this list? What qualities do you have that make you a good friend?

FAKE FRIENDS

Just like anyone else, some disabled people find it really easy to make friends, and some find it more challenging. Some of us have no issues at all finding mates, and others are shy, nervous or unsure of what to say. Plus, as disabled people we can worry that others may be ableist towards us. And sometimes, people can actually have really good intentions, but they might be acting in a way that's ableist without even realizing. All of this can be really confusing, and sometimes it's hard to work out if someone is actually a friend or if they're more of a fake friend.

If you're unsure of whether someone is being a good friend to you, check in with how you feel after you've spent time with them. Do you feel happy and positive about yourself? Or do you feel a bit less like yourself, as though you've had to change who you are to fit with their view of you? If so, they're probably <u>not</u> a good person for you to be friends with.

When I was at school, I found myself sometimes changing my behaviour to try to make other kids like me. I was really good at making people laugh and I thought that maybe if I kept doing that, they would be my friends. Sometimes I would even share gossip about other kids just to impress the ones I wanted to be friends with. But often those kids would enjoy my jokes, or listen to some gossip I shared, then a few minutes later run off and leave me out of the game they were playing. (By the way, sharing gossip just to make other kids like you doesn't really work and is mean. I'm not proud of that.)

It took me a long time to realize that I was changing who I was just to make others like me, and that it wasn't working because I wasn't being my true self. In a world where we all want to fit in and be cool and popular, some kids might be afraid of being friends with a disabled person simply because they're different. That's their problem though, and you should never feel like you need to change yourself to fit in or get people to like you.

It's hard navigating friendships as a disabled kid, and if you can relate to any of these experiences, I'm sending you a big hug or fist bump (whatever you prefer). But there is a positive side to all of this: when faced with disability, people show who they are very quickly, which means YOU get the choice to decide whether YOU want to be friends with them too.

Any kids that treat you differently because they have a problem with your disability have actually done you a favour – because those kids aren't the kind of people you need to be friends with in the first place.

Real friends don't embarrass you in front of others or make fun of you. Real friends aren't rude to you to impress others. Real friends don't ignore you when other kids are around or leave you out of games to look cool. Real friends won't be unkind to your face, or behind your back.

Who wants to be friends with people who do those things, anyway? **Certainly not me!**

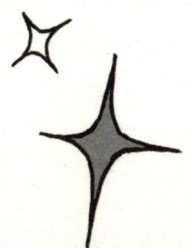

DEALING WITH BULLIES

I wish I didn't need to write this next part and we could all live in a world free from bullying. Unfortunately that's not real life, and we all face unkindness from others sometimes. So it's probably a good idea to talk about it, and if you're someone who experiences bullying, hopefully some of the tips in this chapter will help.

Many kids experience bullying at some point at school, or outside of school at clubs or home, or even just around the neighbour-hood. Bullies aren't very original – they tend to quickly look for something in a person they can make fun of, and disabled kids are very easy targets because we look and/or behave differently to most people around us. It's easy to pick on the boy who is much shorter than all his peers, or the girl who has a speech impediment, for example. Bullies usually behave this way because there is something in their own lives that they are really angry or sad about, and instead of dealing with those feelings they take them out on someone else.

But no matter what someone may be facing in their personal life, making fun of someone else because of the way they look or behave is absolutely not okay.

When I was a kid, I was terrified of bullies (and I still am a bit!). I was shy and I would easily cry, and the last thing I wanted to do was show that their words and actions affected me. So whenever kids were mean to me, I just wouldn't say anything. My face would go red, and I'd blink really quickly to stop the tears from coming. When it happened in school, I sometimes told a teacher. Outside of school, I sometimes told my parents. Sometimes I didn't tell anyone at all – it depended a bit on my mood and whether I actually thought telling an adult would help make me feel better (which it usually did).

If you're someone that has no problem standing up for yourself against bullies, that's brilliant and I'm so proud of you. If you're someone who is scared of bullies like

I was, I'm proud of you too. It's so, so difficult to argue with someone who seems more powerful than you, especially when their words or actions hurt.

Here are some tips for what to do if you ever get into a bad situation with a bully:

Top tip 1 Get away from them as fast as you can

Don't worry about being polite or 'staying strong' – if someone is bullying you, being unkind, or making you feel unsafe, you need to get out of that situation. It's much more important to protect yourself and your emotions. Find someone or a group you trust to surround yourself with, or a quiet, safe space.

Top tip 2 Once you're safely out of the situation, ask yourself what you want to happen next

Do you want a teacher to tell them off, or ask them to apologize? Do you want them to be educated about your disability? Or perhaps you want that person to be kept away from you in lessons or the playground.

Top tip 3 Whatever you want to happen, don't be afraid to ask for it

Once you've decided, tell a trusted adult (teacher, parent, carer, whoever it is) as soon as you can and let them know what you'd like to happen. Please don't ever worry in silence, especially if you feel unsafe. If you have friends you can talk to, that's great, but they can't sort out the situation in the same way an adult can, so please make sure you tell a grown-up too.

Top tip 4 Look after yourself

Afterwards, it can really help to do something lovely for yourself. That could be buying your favourite chocolate bar, texting a friend or spending time watching your favourite movie. Be around people you love who love you back. And always remember, the things bullies say about you are completely untrue and **their nastiness is not about you**.

I hope that you never have to deal with bullies or bullying behaviour, but if you do, I hope these tips help. Make sure you take all the time you need afterwards to process what has happened and talk about it with the people you feel safe with.

You are worthy
of beautiful
friendships that
make you feel

loved,
accepted
and safe.

FRIENDS ARE THERE FOR YOU

Finding disabled friends is great, and having non-disabled friends is great too. Community is so important in helping us to feel supported and loved – and in turn we should support and love our friends back! Wherever or however you make friends – whether it's at school, at a club or activity, in your neighbourhood, via a disability network or online – **I want you to remember...**

 You don't have to be friends with everyone – especially anyone that doesn't treat you right.

 Treat others how you want to be treated! If you show people love and kindness, often they'll return it to you.

 Being open and trusting other people can allow you to build strong friendships.

 In life, we all need help and support from each other. **Even the most successful people didn't get to where they are by themselves** – they had help!

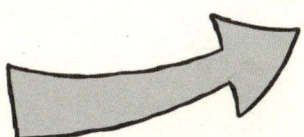

☆ Any 'friends' who make fun of you or ignore you when other people are around aren't real friends. Don't waste your energy on them – **you'll find the right people for you**.

☆ Making friends online can be great, especially if it's hard to find people nearby who share similar experiences to you. But it's important to **remember to stay safe online**, and not to forget that there's a world outside your screens too ☺

☆ Disabled friendships are SO AWESOME – if you don't have any disabled friends yet, **explore opportunities in your area**, or see if there are any conventions for people with your disability like the ones I go to. **You won't automatically be besties with everyone else who is disabled** (just like how we don't get on with everyone who is non-disabled), but it can be wonderful finding people to connect with that understand you in ways most other people can't.

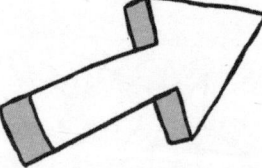

CHAPTER 6

Your Changing Body

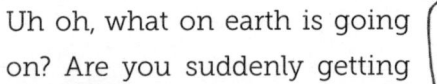

Uh oh, what on earth is going on? Are you suddenly getting your period, spots, body hair, a deeper voice, stubble around your chin, or maybe a bigger Adam's apple? Have you grown taller very quickly? Are you always so sleepy, no matter what time you go to bed? And, oh my gosh, why is everyone suddenly talking about who they fancy All The Time? Don't worry, you're not alone – you're just going through this tiny little thing called puberty.

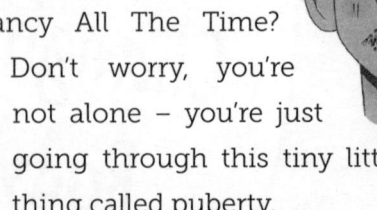

'Puberty, what's *that*?' I hear you cry. Well, it's the process our bodies go through as we grow up and eventually become adults. It usually starts around the age of eleven or twelve, although everyone experiences puberty at different times, and in some cases your disability can affect when you start puberty too. Back in the olden days when I was a teenager, we were taught boys experienced puberty one way, and girls experienced it another. But actually, that's not exactly true: lots of the changes we associate with 'being a boy' – like growing facial hair – can happen for girls too, and vice versa. And of course, the whole 'boys vs girls' thing is so last century anyway (keep reading to learn more about this).

Another thing that we weren't really taught at school was how the body changes we experience during puberty can sometimes create more challenges for disabled kids. In this chapter, we're going to look at some of these changes, including why they happen, what challenges they might create and how to cope with them.

We're also going to talk about something called **body image** – a.k.a. how you feel about your body – and how this can be affected by the changes experienced during puberty. Linked to this is something called your **gender identity**, which is the way you feel about your gender. How you feel about these things can change a lot when you're going through puberty, so it feels like a good time to talk about them. We'll learn from a couple of different disabled people about how these things affected them growing up too.

AHHH, HELP – MY BODY IS CHANGING!

Okay – I know puberty can feel a bit weird, scary and overwhelming at times. And you might be asking yourself, *WHY is all this stuff happening to my brain and body?* Well, it's all because of chemicals in your body called hormones, which are basically like chemical messengers that tell your body what to do. As you start puberty, these hormones start whizzing round your body and setting off lots of changes – such as growing more body hair or developing breasts.

Hormones are the reason why you might suddenly start getting random mood swings too, as those chemicals zooming round your body during puberty can mess with your emotions. Have you seen *Inside Out 2?* That film does a great job of describing what might be happening to your body and in your brain around this time!

Puberty looks different for everyone, but here are some of the key changes that most people – whether they're disabled or not – will experience:

Voice changes. If you have a vulva, your voice might only change a little bit, and if you have a penis, it may get quite a bit deeper – which can take a little while to get used to!

More body hair. This will start growing between your legs and under your arms, and you might notice the hair on your legs, arms and face growing thicker. Sometimes it grows in other places too! While this hair grows for everyone, some people are naturally more or less hairy than others – this is totally normal and nothing to worry about.

Periods. For those that have them, periods usually start anywhere between the ages of ten and sixteen, although some people start having them before or after that. Periods are a sign that your body is changing to make it possible to carry and have babies when you're older. (But it doesn't mean you need to rush into thinking about that though, and it's also totally okay if you don't ever want to have babies.) A period can last between two and seven days, but if they last for longer, are really heavy or really painful, please seek advice from your GP.

Tiredness. I think my pre-teen and teenager years were the most tired I've ever felt! If you've grown up with an older sibling at home, you might be familiar with just how much they seem to sleep all the time. That's because they need rest while all the changes are going on inside their bodies. The same will probably happen to you too.

Mood swings. There are two things that tend to cause mood swings at this age: tiredness (see the last point!), and all those pesky hormones shooting around everywhere. That can mean that sometimes you feel very angry, frustrated or sad – even about small things – and then the next minute you're joyful and happy again. Puberty is a wild ride!

Skin changes. During puberty, your skin starts producing more oil, which can sometimes mean tiny white spots or bigger reddish ones appear on your face (and other parts of your body, like your chest and back).

It can be tempting to pick at these to try to get rid of them, but trust me, that only makes the spots bigger and angrier! It also makes them more likely to leave scars too. Try using a gentle facewash (one that doesn't contain any harsh ingredients – and definitely no teatree or charcoal) and keeping your fingers well away from your face. If you're struggling with skin changes and it's affecting your mood, speak to your adult about booking an appointment with your GP, as they may be able to suggest a treatment to help.

Body changes. As well as all the extra hair, voice and skin changes, you will also start to notice your body changing in other ways. If you have a vulva, then your breasts will usually start to grow around this age, and you may notice your hips getting wider too. If you have a penis, then you'll probably notice it starting to get longer and wider. It can feel strange if your body is changing in ways that are different to your friends, but remember – bodies are different for everyone, and as we already know, looking the same is totally boring.

I know this list probably looks like A LOT of changes.

It's important to remember that everyone's experience of puberty is unique, and everyone goes through different changes at different times.

Some you might not experience at all; some might come on quite slowly, or happen much later – for example, some people won't experience spots or acne during puberty, but might experience them later as an adult. ALL bodies change, and no two bodies are the same. With that in mind, let's look in a bit more detail at some of these changes and how they might affect you, starting with ...

PERIODS!

Please don't be tempted to skip this next bit – even if you're someone who will never have a period, it's important we all understand how they work. And I promise periods aren't as gross and scary as you might think.

Perhaps you've started your period already, or you know other kids who have. Don't worry if you haven't yet – as we talked about before, everyone's periods start at different times.

Before your first period, you might notice some sticky white stuff in your underwear. This is called vaginal discharge (or sometimes just discharge), and it keeps your vagina healthy. Your period will usually start around six months to a year after this discharge and might appear as a brown-ish streak in your underwear. It may be fairly light at first, and likely won't arrive at exactly the same time each month. As time goes on, your periods will get a bit heavier and will appear at roughly the same time every month.

I got my first period when I was thirteen. Some people get theirs before that, and some people get it later. My mum had already told me a bit about periods (I didn't learn *anything* about them in school), and I was excited when it happened. It made me feel really grown up. Hurrah!

Even though I was excited to be part of this new, grown-up club, as time went on, I found it weird how us girls never talked about how our bodies were changing. All the girls at school seemed embarrassed to talk about periods with friends, and we always went to great lengths to hide our pads from each other when we went to the toilet. If you think about it, periods are amazing because they're a sign that your body is changing to allow you to have babies later on (if you want to, though it doesn't guarantee it either). But I quickly discovered that periods weren't something people celebrated – instead, they seemed like something we were ashamed of and embarrassed about.

I also found managing my period challenging sometimes. I leaked a lot (when you get a stain from your period on your underwear or trousers/skirt/dress), and unless I was at home it was often difficult for me to clean myself up. I couldn't face asking anyone to help, because of that whole shame and embarrassment thing I just mentioned. Once when I was a teenager, I ended up with a bright red stain on my WHITE cargo pants – and my friend was too embarrassed to even tell me! I was mortified, especially because the boy I *really* fancied at the time definitely saw ...

AAAARGH!

It was a good few years – maybe not even until I became an adult – before I stopped being embarrassed about my period and the fact that I needed help with it from time to time. Now sometimes my kids help me grab my pads, and we talk about how to manage period care as a disabled person. I want them – and you! – to know that having periods is normal and okay, and that our changing bodies are nothing to be ashamed of. And also that accidents happen to everyone.

The shame around periods is another one of those made-up beliefs in our society that says certain types of bodies and the ways they work are a problem. Sounds a lot like ableism really, doesn't it? But things are changing, as more and more people are encouraging others to shed the shame around periods. In fact, there's a whole movement called the **Period Positivity Movement** that aims to make talking about periods feel normal, and even something to be proud of. You can find out more about it online if you want to (head to the resources section at the back of this book for more info!).

How to be Period Prepared

There are lots of things you can use to manage your periods. Some are trickier to access for people with different disabilities, so it's important to try things out and find what works best for you. Here are some of the different period products you can try:

Period pants. These are just big knickers that have padding built into them. They're usually black to prevent stains. You can put them in the wash and reuse them until they fall apart, just like regular clothes!

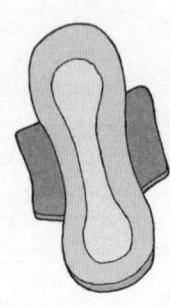

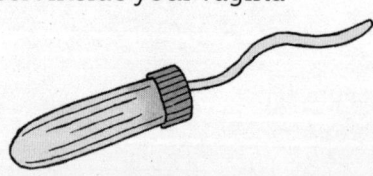

Pads or towels. A wad of material that soaks up blood: one side is soft against your skin, and the other side sticks to the inside of your underwear. You can buy reusable ones, which you put in the wash after each use, and disposable ones that you just use once.

Tampons. A small cylinder made from cotton that you insert inside your vagina to soak up blood. Applicator tampons come in a little tube that helps you to push the tampon into your vagina, but there are also non-applicator ones that you can insert with just your finger. After a couple of hours – depending on how heavy your period is – you pull a little string on the end of the tampon to take it out and change it.

Menstrual cups. A small, cup-like device made of rubber or plastic. You push it up into your vagina and it collects blood. After a few hours, you'll need to take it out and change or wash it.

Once you've worked out which period product(s) you prefer, it might be helpful to pack a small period bag to carry around with you – this will help you to feel prepared and in control in case of any sudden surprises. It could also include a spare change of underwear in case you leak.

If you're someone that won't experience periods, thank you for reading this part. It's useful for people who don't bleed to know what happens to those of us that do – it means that we can all be kinder and more understanding towards each other. In the same way, it's important for non-disabled kids to be aware that disabled kids will have needs that are different to theirs, and to offer support where they can. If all of us could understand each other's bodies a bit better, then maybe we wouldn't feel embarrassed **to ask for help when we need it.**

WHY AM I SO TIRED ALL THE TIME?

You might've started to notice that you're struggling to wake up in the morning, or maybe finding it hard not to nod off midway through Wednesday's double history lesson. A lot of that is down to your body needing to rest because it's growing and changing so quickly. Plus you might have long hours at school; there's homework and after-school activities; and at this age you might find it hard to fall asleep at night too.

Even though all teens and pre-teens get tired, when I was that age, I was definitely a bit sleepier than my peers. I didn't really understand it at the time, but now I realize it was because my disabled body uses up a lot of energy trying to keep up with others. Take walking, for example. Because I walk slowly and my steps are small, I usually have to take twice as many steps as an average-height person, which kinda sorta feels like I'm walking twice as far.

Perhaps you've also experienced feeling more tired or having less energy than your peers. There are lots of reasons why disabled people often struggle with energy levels – for example, it could be that you have difficulty concentrating for long periods of time, or that you need to take regular breaks from screens to avoid headaches. And the added pressure that puberty puts on our bodies can make us feel even more tired.

So for those of us who are sleepyheads, you'll find my top tips for dealing with tiredness, fatigue and low energy levels, to avoid burnout over the page.

? **Burnout:** we experience burnout when our bodies and minds have been working too hard for too long. This often results in us being extremely tired and/or getting sick and being unable to do regular activities for a while, until we slow down and look after ourselves a bit more gently.

Top tip 1 Prioritize

This means working out which things you need to do, which things you want to do, and what could be left until another day. Once you figure out your priorities (the things you need to do), you can start managing your energy levels. You can't do everything, and that's okay.

Top tip 2 Pace yourself

One way I tackle everything I need to do is by going slowly! If I try to do tasks quickly, I get tired, so I'm more likely to leave things unfinished. If I work slowly, with breaks in between, I have more chance of being able to complete my tasks properly. The classic story of 'The Hare and Tortoise' is a great reminder that being fast doesn't necessarily mean we win the race.

Top tip 3 Say no

I've said this before, but we can never be reminded enough: say no when you need to. You don't have to do everything, and you're not a failure for needing to stop and rest. If your body is calling on you to let it rest, listen to it.

Top tip 4 Talk to someone

Tell your adult(s) if you're struggling with managing your time and energy levels and see if you can figure out a schedule that works better for you. Maybe you need to stop swimming for a bit while you're studying for tests, or maybe going to your friend's house on a Sunday evening wouldn't be the wisest choice. You could even write out a realistic schedule for yourself and stick it on the fridge. Check in with your adult regularly and talk about how things are going and whether you need to make any adjustments.

We think of puberty as part of the process of growing up and becoming more independent. But for disabled kids going through puberty, growing up can actually mean we need a bit more help than we used to – at least at first – as we might be faced with a brand-new set of challenges to figure out as our bodies develop, including increased tiredness.

It can feel weird to notice our friends need less support, while we need more or the same amount. But I want you to remember that being more independent isn't a sign that you are more 'successful' at life or grown up. Being a person who can clearly identify and communicate when you need support is grown up too. Being unable to do something, or unable do it yet, is absolutely fine.

No matter what
you can or can't do,
it doesn't make you any
less ready to grow up.

CHANGES TO YOUR INTIMATE PARTS (A.K.A. BREASTS, TESTICLES, PENISES AND MORE!)

No giggling at this next bit, please. I know breasts, testicles and penises might seem funny, but it's important to understand the body changes that you and your peers might be going through at this age.

As mentioned earlier in the chapter, your intimate body parts usually grow during puberty. If you have a vagina, you will start developing breasts around the ages of nine to eleven, although it can be earlier or later than this. Not all breasts develop in the same way. Some get bigger quickly, while others grow slowly over time. You might have nipples that are inverted (or point inwards), and for some people their breasts don't change much at all. You might also notice more fat appearing around your upper arms, thighs and bum, and that your hips get wider.

If you have testicles (also known as balls) and a penis, your penis will usually start to grow longer and wider between the ages of eleven to fifteen, (although again, everyone is different). During this time, you might also start to experience wet dreams – this is when your penis releases semen (the cream-coloured fluid that contains sperm) during your sleep. This is totally normal and nothing to be embarrassed about. Other changes that you might notice are a bigger Adam's apple (the lump at the front of your neck), and more body fat around your stomach.

It can feel strange seeing your breasts or penis take on a new shape, and you might wonder what they'll end up looking like. It's good to be curious and to learn about what goes on both inside and outside your skin. What's not okay is to make fun of someone for the way their body is changing.

There was one boy at my secondary school who made fun of my breasts. They were already pretty big by the time I was eleven, and their growth wasn't slowing down! I used to feel embarrassed by them, and that boy's mean jokes only made it worse. Why exactly are big boobs funny though? They're not – they're just lumps of tissue and fat on the body. Penises aren't funny either, no matter what size or shape they are. In fact, nothing about our bodies is funny.

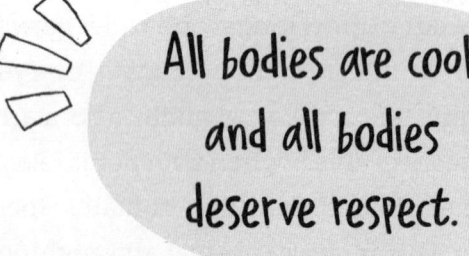

All bodies are cool, and all bodies deserve respect.

If you notice any kids making jokes about how other kids' bodies look, you could say, 'Hey, all bodies are different, including yours! So why are you making jokes about someone else's?'

WHY IS EVERYONE SUDDENLY FLIRTING WITH EACH OTHER?

If puberty wasn't enough to deal with already, you might have noticed that suddenly your friends are all obsessed with talking about who they fancy. Or maybe you've spotted other kids acting strangely around each other, like trying to impress them loads? Welcome to the world of flirting.

Now you might already be a pro at flirting yourself, or maybe you find it totally weird or scary. However you feel about it, that's cool and it's important to remember that everyone is changing at their own pace.

My experiences with flirting at this age weren't great – I tried, but it always felt *so* awkward, and the kids I liked made it very clear that they didn't fancy me back. It really upset me at the time because it felt like they didn't like the way I looked, and I wish I could've realized that their opinions didn't change the fact that I have an awesome personality and a good heart. Both of those qualities are way more important than appearance anyway!

If you're worried about whether anyone is ever going to like you romantically, you're not alone. So many of us worry about that – whether we are disabled or not. I know it can be REALLY annoying when adults tell you, 'It will happen when you're older!', especially when you're in school and you feel like you might get left behind if you don't do all the exciting things your friends are doing. But it is so, SO important to only start dating when you are comfortable doing so, and with people who feel good to be around. And if you feel like:

No-one is ever going to fancy me!

Please know that:

A) your feelings are valid, but

B) it almost definitely isn't true, and

C) we all struggle with this feeling sometimes – even us adults!

When you're older you won't care – or really remember – *when* these things happened; you'll care about whether they were good experiences or not. Take your time.

FEELING DISCONNECTED FROM YOUR BODY

With all the changes that you're going through during puberty, it's normal to sometimes feel a bit weirded out by or disconnected from your body. When my boobs started growing, I started to feel like they weren't really part of me – they were just these big, strange objects attached to my chest. Have you ever felt like that about a part of your body – like it's not really yours, or doesn't look how you expected it to?

It took me a while to accept all the bits of my changing disabled body. I remember feeling embarrassed about my toes – my fourth toe is squished on top of the third and fifth toe, which is common for many people with achondroplasia dwarfism. It was another reminder of my disability, and I hated that it looked different to other people's, so I used to avoid taking my socks off around other kids.

Perhaps you've tried to hide a part of your disability before? If you have, you're certainly not alone and lots of disabled people go through this, especially during our teenage years. You might remember Joy from Chapter 4, who was embarrassed to be seen using her cane at school. It can be hard to feel confident about our different bodies and the aids we use to help us, and this can get *even harder* when your body is suddenly going through lots of changes and the last thing you want is to stand out.

Another word for feeling disconnected from your body is disassociation. This is the feeling of being separate from your body or the world around you, so it can seem like what's happening to you isn't real. I used to feel like this a lot as a teen, though at the time, I didn't know the proper word for it. I called it feeling 'soupy' – sounds strange I know, but to me it made sense, like my body was this weird soup that my mind was swimming around in!

One of the ways I eventually managed to overcome those strange feelings and create a more positive body image was by taking care of the parts I felt disconnected from. So here are my top tips for navigating body changes:

Top tip 1 Taking care of your body

Looking after your body through acts of self-care – such as washing and drying yourself or applying a body cream – can make you feel more connected to it. If you're someone who needs help with any of these things, perhaps you could speak to your adult about how you'd prefer to do them now that you're getting a bit older. For example, could they step out of the room for ten minutes once they've helped you get into the bath? Or could they help you have a go at applying cream by yourself? (There are also some tricks and tools you could use to make any tasks easier.) Having some time to care for your body, however you choose to do this, is important. Even if caring for it simply means lying in bed a bit longer!

Top tip 2 Your body, your style!

Wearing clothes that make you feel comfortable and that express who you are can help you feel confident and in control of your body. If accessing shops is hard for you, you could ask your adult to check which shops have wheelchair-accessible changing rooms, or go shopping at less busy times of day. Shopping online is also a great option, as the internet offers more disability-inclusive brands than the typical shopping centre. Have a look together with your adult for clothing that feels good and works well for you.

Top tip 3 Setting body boundaries

It's really important to communicate when you're okay with other people touching you, and when you're not. It can be tricky when you've relied on adults a lot to help with personal care to feel able to say something like, 'Actually, I want to try doing this myself' or 'Please don't do it that way, I would prefer . . . ' It's up to you to decide how you want adults to help you, or when to have a go by yourself. And it's also really normal to find things difficult at first, or to take time to develop a technique for things like putting on clothes or doing your hair by yourself. The most important thing is that you feel comfortable with your adults' involvement in caring for you, and that you feel able to say no when you want to.

Top tip 4 Spend time with your reflection

When I was a teenager, I avoided looking in the mirror because the way my body looked didn't really fit with how I saw myself. If this is something that you find hard too, then try finding a quiet spot to look at your reflection from time to time, even if it's just for a few seconds. While you're doing that, focus on something about your reflection that you like. Maybe you're wearing your favourite top, or you have a cool hairstyle today. Maybe you like your shoes, your eye colour, or the way the outfit looks on you. Whatever it is – no matter how small – recognize something positive about the way you look. If you do this exercise regularly enough, it might just help you to feel more confident and happier in your body.

Over the years, I've come to accept my body, and my 'soup' has slowly joined together to become something more solid (like a sandwich? Okay, maybe I've overused the food visuals now . . .) I feel less disassociated and more joined up, like my body is something I can control and take comfort in. It's not always easy, and sometimes I still have my soupy days. So if you feel *kinda sorta not great* about your body sometimes, I want you to know that this is okay. Making time to look after your body – especially when you're going through all the tough stuff that puberty throws at you – is so important and can help you to manage those feelings.

GENDER STEREOTYPES

Puberty is confusing enough already, but on top of all that, you might notice a sudden pressure to look or act a certain way depending on your gender. Perhaps you've felt like your gender doesn't always fit with who you are, or that you don't like the things that boys or girls are 'supposed' to like. When I was growing up, I sometimes felt like the label 'girl' didn't really fit me. If 'girl' was a circle, I felt like I was sort of on the edge – not outside the circle, but not bang in the middle either. In other words, I didn't often feel very girly.

This whole idea that boys or girls are 'supposed' to like certain things or look a certain way is based on **gender stereotypes**. These are made-up beliefs that define what boys and girls are meant to be, say, do and enjoy, just because of the body they were born into.

For example, all boys . . .

⭐ must be good at football or other competitive sports,
⭐ have blue, black or red as their favourite colour,
⭐ must be strong in every way,
⭐ must not cry or talk about feelings,
⭐ are called 'tough', 'handsome' and 'clever';

while all girls ...

⭐ must enjoy playing with dolls,
⭐ have pink or purple as their favourite colour,
⭐ talk about their feelings, and cry when
   they're upset,
⭐ wear dresses, heels, jewellery and make-up,
⭐ are called 'pretty' and 'beautiful'.

Can you think of any other gender stereotypes you've come across?

Of course, these stereotypes are all *rubbish* – we can all be a mix of these things, or other things entirely, whatever our gender. But sometimes, navigating the expectations that come with gender stereotypes can be tricky, especially if you're disabled and you already look and feel different to the people around you.

What does gender mean to you?

Maybe, like me, you've sometimes felt like your gender doesn't fit with who are. Or maybe you're totally comfortable with it, or you're still figuring it all out. There's no right way to feel about or express your gender, no matter what society might sometimes tell you. Whatever your personal journey is, there's no rush, and no matter what, who you are and how you feel is valid and deserving of love and respect.

If you are feeling worried about your body, your gender identity or both, it's really important to speak to a trusted adult if you are able to and not manage these feelings by yourself.

As I mentioned in the introduction to this chapter, gender identity actually goes way beyond those boy/girl stereotypes. You could be a boy, girl, non-binary or something else entirely, and your feelings about your gender could shift and change. There are lots of ways we can feel about our gender identity, and we call this the **gender spectrum**.

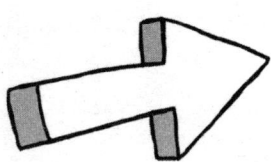

Non-binary: having a gender identity that isn't male or female.

Genderfluid: having a gender identity that can shift and change at any time.

Queer: a term describing any sexual orientation and/or gender identity that may fall outside the common types. Some people use 'queer' to describe anyone in the LGBTQAI+ community, but not everyone in the community does, so it's always best to check what term people prefer.

I spoke to my friend Max, who is queer, non-binary and disabled, about their journey towards accepting their gender identity, as well as their disability.

I think my first instance of dysphoria was feeling like I wasn't like the 'other girls'. I was bullied at school because I didn't like what the other girls liked, and I didn't really fit in. The more I tried to fit into the box of being a girl, the worse I felt. It was many years before I figured out that the reason I wasn't like the other girls was because I just wasn't a girl at all.

Dysphoria: a sense of unhappiness with life. For people who experience gender dysphoria, this can mean they feel unhappy with the gender the world tells them they are.

As well as trying to fit in as 'just another girl', Max also said they often tried hard to act non-disabled, but it didn't always work.

While trying really hard to be a girl, I wore heels to school, which weirdly helped some of the pain I was having in my hips, but they also made me slower, clumsier and louder. I was trying very hard to be an able-bodied girl, when I wasn't either of those things. As hard as I tried to hide who I was, I was still disabled, I was still queer, and I was still non-binary. But as soon as I started to lean into those things and explore who I really was, the more I found my community and the more I fit in.

Whatever your relationship is with your gender, and your disabled identity, I hope that, like Max, you have space to explore those parts of you that make you different. Once you learn to accept those bits of your identity, you'll find that others start to accept you for who you are too.

GENDER AND BEAUTY IDEALS

One of the reasons why I didn't really feel like a girl growing up was because I was taught that girls look a certain way, and I just didn't look like that. I didn't have blonde hair and blue eyes, long legs or a flat tummy. I couldn't wear high heels, and I wasn't ever really into make-up or short skirts.

Now, this image of what a girl 'should' look like (slim, blonde etc) is what's known as a **beauty ideal**. Beauty ideals are another way society has of telling us which bodies are 'good' and which aren't. They are based on different forms of prejudice, including **racism** (which says that white people are more important than Black, Brown and Indigenous people), **fatphobia** (which says that slim bodies are better than fat ones), and, of course, our old enemy, **ableism**. To add to this list of totally rubbish made-up beliefs, there is also **transphobia**. This prejudice says that bodies that don't follow the very narrow rules of gender stereotypes – bodies that are

also called **gender non-conforming** – are less valuable (again, this is totally untrue).

Remember the word we learned in Chapter 1 that describes all the different parts of our identity, and how we can have many parts that are all connected? Yes – intersectionality is what we're talking about here.

All of these types of prejudice put together create a beauty ideal that says white, slim, non-disabled and gender-conforming bodies are the most beautiful and valuable. Of course, you and I know that we're *ALL* beautiful, and we're all valuable. But if you've ever felt unhappy with the way you look, or pressured to look a certain way, those beauty ideals have probably got something to do with it. They can make all of us feel like we're not good enough sometimes.

It can be hard to avoid beauty ideals because they are literally everywhere – TV, advertizing, films, magazines and online. Plus, beauty brands want you to believe that their products will help you achieve that perfect beautiful body, even though such a thing doesn't really exist. So if you're ever tempted to try a make-up or beauty product, try asking yourself, 'Do I actually want to wear that thing? Or have I been convinced that it'll somehow make me look better?' A product or device will never make you 'more beautiful' because . . .

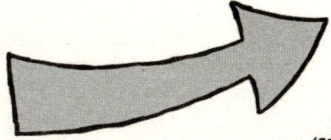

Our beauty isn't
defined by how we look.
It's about who we are inside.

Finding power in your beauty

With all that said, it can be fun to experiment with and enjoy beauty products and gadgets if that's something you're interested in. I like wearing lip gloss and putting wax in my hair to make it spiky, for example. Playing around with make-up and beauty can be a way of expressing your creativity, exploring your gender identity, and figuring out what makes you feel good from the inside out.

My friend Katouche is a huge fan of beauty products – in fact, one of her jobs is to tell people about new beauty products that come out:

I love everything to do with beauty – make-up, fashion, clothing, hair; I love the power beauty has to tell a story about who we are and how we want to show up in the world.

As a Black disabled woman, enjoying using beauty products and wearing great clothes is important to Katouche, as she says it helps her to feel more in control of who she is:

> *When you're disabled and Black, people can already have so many ideas of who you are and whether or not you're important. Being able to dictate what I wear and how I express myself is my way of taking back some of that power.*

Yes, Katouche! I really think clothes and beauty products can make us feel so powerful. Clothes have definitely helped me to figure out who I am and feel comfortable in the way I look. I used to wear a lot of grey clothing with no patterns on but gradually, as I've grown more confident, I've added more colour, more funky designs and *even* some sequins to my wardrobe. Wearing comfortable clothes that I love makes me feel confident in myself and my own unique sense of style.

Perhaps you have special clothes in your wardrobe that make you feel super confident and cool when you put them on, or maybe you love experimenting with colourful make-up, accessories or jewellery? However you choose to express yourself, finding beauty and fashion styles you love can be a powerful way of showing the world who you are.

IT'S NORMAL TO BE DIFFERENT

One thing that helps me when I'm feeling low and like nobody thinks I'm cool or pretty or whatever is remembering that we're all different in some way. Sure, I might have been the only kid with achondroplasia dwarfism at my school, and I had the biggest boobs, but that didn't mean everyone else looked the same and were never made fun of. **I wasn't the only one that looked different.** There were kids at my school who were bullied because of their weight, their race, their family set-up, their religion . . . and many were also teased for smaller things like their hairstyle, what they wore or whether they had the latest gadget. Let's face it – *bullies will literally find anything to pick on*. A kid I know was once made fun of because they didn't have the same water bottle as their friends!

The boy that teased me about my chest was unkind to quite a few of us, but I realized later his life was far from perfect, and he had probably been really unhappy.

There were kids at my school who I thought had had an easy, happy life, but they had a horrible time at home, or didn't have enough money for what they needed, or had other problems I knew nothing about. That doesn't excuse their mean behaviour, but it does help to remember that nobody's life is perfect and everyone struggles with some stuff.

The reality is nobody has a perfect life, a perfect brain or a perfect body. People often say there's no such thing as normal, and they're right.

There is only ONE of each of us in the world. We are all unique, and that's incredible.

And we all experience puberty and growing up slightly differently. So if ever someone tries to make you feel bad for the way you look, just remember – you're on the right track, because it's normal to be different.

All bodies change, and all bodies are beautiful.

Here are some things to remember about puberty, growing up and your body:

⭐ Everyone experiences puberty differently, and **everyone's experiences are valid**.

⭐ Just like there's no such thing as normal, there's also **no such thing as perfect**. Nobody looks perfect, and nobody experiences their body changing in a perfect way.

⭐ Your body might feel strange as it grows. Most people feel similar to you. **Look after your body**, and in time you might feel more ownership and acceptance of those bits you're not sure about.

⭐ You are allowed to **express your gender however you want to**.

⭐ **It's okay to need more support as your body is changing**, e.g. if you're struggling with tiredness. Talk to your adults about what they can do to help lighten the load.

If you're worried about romance and dating and all that stuff, you're not alone – **others just might not be talking about it**. If you feel it would help, try opening up to a friend, an older sibling or parent/carer, to see what they think.

What's in people's hearts is far more important than how they look.

If you're struggling with feelings about your gender as your body changes, it's okay not to have that all figured out straight away. **What's important is that you feel able to express yourself in the way you feel most comfortable**. And make sure you talk to an adult you trust if those feelings become too tough to deal with by yourself.

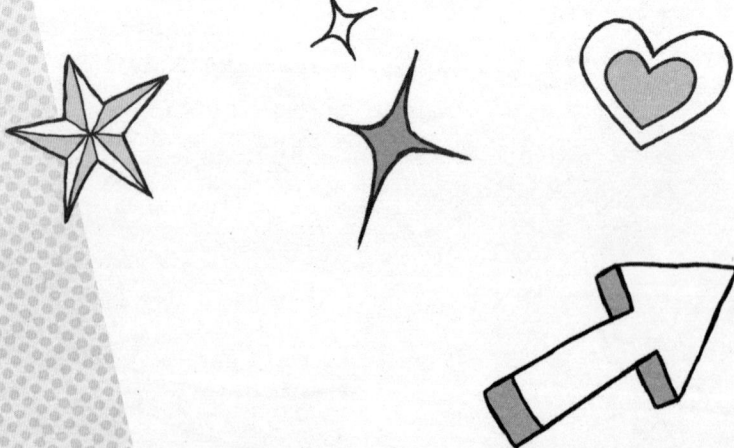

CHAPTER 7

Hospitals, Doctors and All That Medical Stuff

Can you remember your last hospital or medical appointment? Maybe it was in the last year, month or even week? If you are disabled, then the likelihood is that you'll be able to remember at least one recent appointment. You may even be very familiar with the paint colour on the waiting-room walls . . .

Your parent or carer has likely got all your doctors' and specialists' office numbers saved into their phone, and you've probably had to skip some lessons at school to attend appointments, tests and check-ups.

Whether you're in and out of hospitals, doctor's surgeries, specialist centres or see a healthcare professional at home, this chapter is for you. Disabled kids can often have LOTS of appointments – which is great in one way (we get to skip double science, hurrah!), but sometimes all of the back and forth, waiting around and being asked loads of questions can be a real pain in the neck. Not to mention the quite strange things medical staff can say at times too . . .

THE WAITING ROOM

Have you ever sat in a waiting room for what feels like hours on end? I remember doing that a lot as a kid. The walls were always white or yellow, and there were usually some old children's toys in the corner and women's magazines from five years ago on the table. The chairs were uncomfortable, and my legs would often hurt if I sat on them for too long. Thirty years later, most waiting rooms I visit still look the same – though sometimes they do also have a TV now!

I didn't love waiting rooms, because the longer I was in them, the more anxious I became about my appointment. I also felt anxious in waiting rooms because sometimes a doctor would come over and tell my parents something about my health that they were worried about (often in front of the whole room – cheers, doc!).

Anxiety: how we feel when our tummies are all wobbly inside and we are very worried about something. Anxiety, or feeling anxious, might cause us not to sleep very well, to be extra grumpy or shy, and/or to fidget or move around lots, or bite our nails.

Sometimes it was better not to think about bad news or what could go wrong, just before an appointment. It definitely didn't help to be stressed with worry when it was finally my turn to go into the doctor's office. Having things to do while I waited helped me to distract myself and prevent any anxiety from building. Some of the things I used to enjoy doing to pass the time while I was waiting around were:

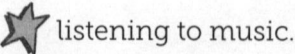 reading my favourite magazine or doing puzzles in my puzzle book. (I loved wordsearches!)

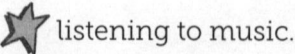 listening to music.

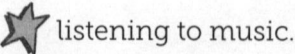 playing small games, like cards, with whoever was with me.

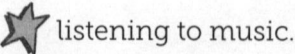 drawing, doodling or writing to someone. (I was obsessed with writing to pen pals when I was a kid.)

 doing homework. (Okay, this one might be less fun – but it can be a useful time to get it out of the way ...)

 EATING SNACKS!

What do you enjoy doing to pass the time? It requires a bit of planning ahead to make sure these things are available to us when we need them, especially if we're in an environment like a waiting room that doesn't have much to play with or do in it. If you don't already have one, it might be a good idea to have a special bag just for those times you need something to distract you. Stuff it with your favourite bits and take it with you to appointments, on long car rides, and any other environments you usually have to wait around in.

IN THE DOCTOR'S OFFICE

Okay, now you're finally heading into the doctor's office – it's your time to shine! Time to tell the doctor what you might be struggling with and what you need them to do. But argh, you've got sweaty hands, and the noises and smells and lights are so overwhelming that you've forgotten everything that was in your head – you go to open your mouth but the words don't come out! Sound familiar? You might be experiencing sensory overload.

> **?**
>
> **Sensory overload:** when one or more of your five senses (touch, sight, hearing, smell or taste) are overwhelmed with too much information and create more feelings than you can handle.

If you've been in that situation before, you're not alone. Lots of people find doctor's offices kinda sorta stressful, and it can often feel like as soon as you're in there, you immediately forget everything you wanted to say. When I was young, I was anxious a lot of the time and I didn't like speaking to people I didn't know, especially about my personal care or my worries. Trying to open up in a place where I didn't feel comfortable felt extra hard.

Most of the time, the doctors I met were kind, friendly, respectful and talked to me directly, not my parents. They did everything they could to make me feel relaxed and supported. Doctors and nurses want to help – after all, that's why they're in the job they're in. But sometimes medical staff were less friendly or only talked to my parents, even though I was old enough and capable of answering their questions myself. And occasionally I had felt really uncomfortable – like when a doctor was examining me and invited student nurses and doctors to come and watch without checking with me first. I felt like saying,

Excuse me, I'm not a museum exhibit, I'm a PERSON!

I hope that all your medical experiences are positive, but if you feel like your appointment hasn't gone the way you wanted it to, or a doctor hasn't really listened to you, I want you to know it is never your fault. Sometimes doctors and nurses can get things wrong. This might be because they are stressed and under pressure, or because they don't have experience of caring for someone with your particular disability. Whatever the reason, that doesn't mean it's okay. That's why it's really important that you're able to speak up for yourself as much as you can, so that your needs can be met. It helps medical staff to learn how to do things differently next time! Doctors might know lots of things and have super-smart brains and stuff, but they don't know what it's like to be you. They can guess, and they can learn from what you say, but they don't have that unique, direct experience. If you're unhappy with or unsure about something to do with your care, it's so important that you feel able to speak up and talk about it so you can find a plan you are happy with.

THERE ARE NEVER TOO MANY QUESTIONS!

Sometimes it can be tricky as a young person to know how and when to say, 'No, that's not for me'. Of course, it's very important to listen to doctors, but ultimately these are your decisions – because they're happening to your body – and you deserve to have your choices heard and respected.

But in order to make the decision that's right for you, you first need to understand what exactly is going on inside your body and brain, and what they want to do to help you. Sometimes the way doctors and nurses talk can be really confusing and hard to follow (even for adults), so it's important to ask questions if you don't understand something or need more information.

If you ever feel confused or overwhelmed about anything to do with your medical care, here are some things you might want to ask or say to your doctors and nurses to help you feel more in control and able to make decisions:

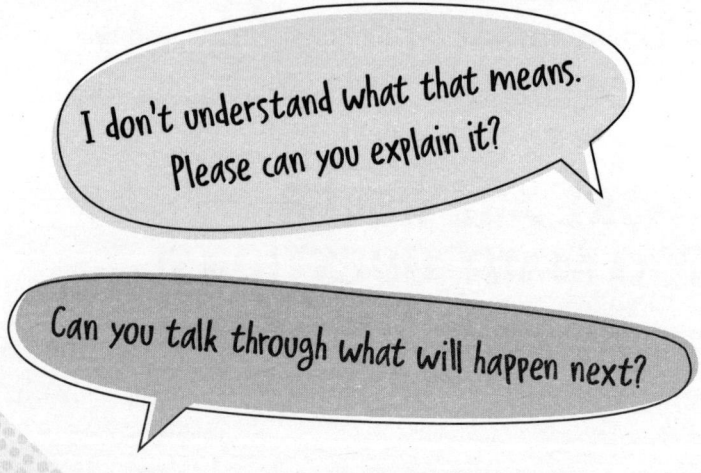

I don't understand what that means. Please can you explain it?

Can you talk through what will happen next?

Why is my body doing that?

If I say yes, will I have to do [XYZ]?
If I say no, what other options are there?

What are the side effects[3] of that treatment?

Please could you tell me more about . . .

Yes, I'm okay with that. Or,
no, I'm not comfortable with that.

I'm not sure about [XYZ] . . .
I think I need some more time to decide.

3. A side effect is how certain medicine makes you feel when you take it – for example, some medicines can make you feel sick or give you a headache.

That last one is super important. Sometimes you can't decide this kind of stuff right away and you might need a bit more time to think. That's okay! You should never feel rushed into any medical decisions. You may need to go home, do your own research, talk to the adults in your life and decide in your own time. You are allowed to wait however long it takes to feel comfortable to give your consent.

Consent: a form of permission that we give someone else to do something. For example, you might say yes – in other words, give your consent – when you visit the doctor with a sore throat and they ask if they can examine your tongue.

Remember, nobody has the right to do anything to, make decisions about or touch your body (except in an emergency) without your consent – or, if you're unable to answer, the consent of the adult you're with. Even doctors. So it's down to you to speak up if something isn't right for you and you need it to change.

Here are my top tips for managing medical appointments:

Top tip 1 Plan ahead

Talk to your adult(s) beforehand and have a think about the things the medical staff might say or ask you. Make a plan for how to tackle those conversations: do you want your adult to speak on your behalf, or would you prefer to talk to the doctors yourself? Share any concerns with your adult, along with anything you'd like them to help you say during the appointment. The doctors might ignore you and speak to the adult first, but if your adult knows you'd like to speak for yourself, they can help make sure the other adults in the room listen to you.

Top tip 2 Do your own research

If you or your adult know other people with your disability or disabilities, you could ask them if they have had the same experiences as you and if so, how they managed. Alongside your adult, research your disability and the treatment options online in order to find out more about what's happening to you and some of the things the doctors might say in advance. It's important to remember that treatments can vary from person to person and between different doctors though, so try to stay open-minded in your appointments. What works for someone else won't necessarily work for you, but it's good to know your options.

Top tip 3 Ask as many questions as you want!

If you don't understand something or want to know more, ask the medical staff to explain – or ask your adult to find out for you. There's no question too small or silly. Knowing exactly what's going on with your care plan is super helpful because that way there won't be any unwelcome surprises.

Top tip 4 Remember that doctors, nurses and medical staff are human beings too

They're not perfect and they get it wrong sometimes, just like we do. So sometimes we need to give them a break. That doesn't mean we shouldn't ask questions or make sure we are happy with our care; it's just about remembering that everyone in the situation is probably trying their best, so be kind to each other.

Top tip 5 Reward yourself with a treat after your appointment

My friend Dom told me about how on his hospital visits, he would always go for a treat before or afterwards with his mum.

> I was born with brittle bone disease, which means my bones break more easily, and I'm short like Cathy too. I use a powered wheelchair to whizz around and get me from A to B. Since birth, I have had lots of regular appointments at hospitals and clinics, including a big operation on my spine. For me, hospital visits were often adventures into London, where no doubt I got to eat a bit more ice cream than normal! I made sure to bring my favourite things, and my mum planned some nice things for us to do before and after.

Of course, treats don't always have to be food-related (although those are pretty great). It could be a relaxing bath, seeing your friends or playing your favourite game. Whatever you enjoy!

MY BODY/BRAIN DOESN'T NEED FIXING, THANK YOU VERY MUCH!

The job of your doctor and other healthcare professionals is to make you feel better and to fix medical problems where possible. Now, often that's a good thing. For example, if you experience severe headaches and are given medicine that helps take the pain away – great! Or if you need glasses so you can see better, that's a nice easy fix too.

But when the fix is more about making your body look or function like everyone else's, and isn't something that will cure pain or accessibility issues you're having, the decision on whether or not to go ahead with it can feel a bit more complicated. This goes back to the medical model that we looked at in Chapter 1 – a.k.a. the theory that our bodies and brains are A Problem That Needs To Be Fixed.

The way medicine is taught to doctors and healthcare staff often focuses on finding ways to cure patients, and this approach can be damaging to disabled people because disability isn't something that can simply be cured. Of course, you and I know disability is *not* a problem to be fixed, but because we all live and work in an ableist society, sometimes healthcare professionals need to be reminded!

When I was growing up, there was this treatment called limb lengthening available for children with achondroplasia dwarfism. It's a very slow and extremely painful process, and a BIG decision to say yes to.

Once I was the age you are now, my doctors started talking about limb lengthening and asking if I wanted to have it. I already knew other people with my disability who were going through the process and it looked so painful. And the thing is, it's not even something that totally 'fixes' us – we still have dwarfism, and we still look like we have it – it just makes us a bit taller. So having limb lengthening would help me to reach a higher supermarket shelf, but it wouldn't get rid of any potential problems I might have with my back, or any other medical issues. It also wouldn't stop ableism from happening to me because I would still look, and be, disabled. To me, limb lengthening has always felt like a procedure focused on making people with dwarfism look more 'normal' (and as you know, I quite like the fact that I'm not!). So I said no to the surgery, and I've never regretted that decision.

It's totally each kid's individual choice, with help and advice from their adults, whether to have these sorts of operations. There are lots of reasons people say 'yes', and they're all valid. There are also lots of reasons people say 'no'.

We should all be given the chance to decide what happens to us, and not everyone is going to choose the same path as me – or you. And that's okay!

When I was your age, I sometimes did wish life was easier for me – that I didn't look different and that I could do the same things as my friends. I wished that I was able to walk down the street as fast as my mates and have nobody stare at me.

But, even though being disabled frustrated me sometimes, it felt like such a huge part of who I was that I couldn't imagine trying to get rid of it. I didn't want to go through all that pain of limb lengthening to try to hide that part of myself away.

I think deep down I knew that, **for me to be happy, I needed to work on fully accepting who I was, inside and out.**

After all, I was already on my own personal journey to being kinda sorta okay with being disabled. And that was exactly where I needed to be.

INTERVIEW WITH A REAL-LIFE DISABLED DOCTOR!

My friend Hannah is a doctor AND she's disabled (yeah, she's very cool!). She has kindly answered some of my questions about being a disabled doctor, and about how best to communicate with doctors as disabled patients.

Please introduce yourself and your work

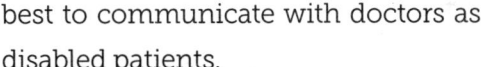

I'm Hannah and I'm a GP, which stands for 'General Practitioner'. This means I look after everybody – from tiny babies right the way through to people who are really elderly. I like to think of it as 'family medicine' because there's no-one I won't see!

What made you want to become a doctor?

When I was growing up, I saw doctors doing amazing things to look after my brothers, who were both very unwell. I realized that they weren't just looking after my brothers though – they cared for my entire family. I wanted to look after people, but not just looking at their illnesses. I wanted to look after them as complex, messy human beings, because we are all more than just an illness or a disability!

What perspective do you think being a disabled doctor gives you when you're supporting disabled and ill patients?

When disabled patients see me sat in my wheelchair, or using different tools to support my ADHD, they can see that I'm like them in some way, and that I probably 'get it'. I know a lot of the challenges disabled people face, particularly in terms of getting healthcare, so I try to make things better for my disabled community.

What advice do you have for disabled kids navigating lots of appointments, surgeries and all that fun stuff?

Lists help me a LOT. Sometimes it can be daunting when you are going to see a doctor: you may feel rushed, or everything you wanted to ask can fall out of your head. I love it when my patients come with a list to work through with me – even if we can't deal with it all in one appointment, we can prioritize things together and make a plan for next time. Also, taking someone you trust with you can be really helpful – ideally someone who'll let you talk as much as you want to.

What are some positive things about how the medical world is changing for disabled people?

More and more disabled people are becoming doctors – so more and more of us are out there to look after you, and our non-disabled colleagues are learning from us too! There is a lot of support as you transition from the Children's Teams into Adult Care, and we are much better at ensuring you are heard [than we used to be].

Hannah's right – the medical world is so much better than it used to be for disabled people. I now have much better medical experiences than I did growing up, and I see that with my own children too – they are given more power in their appointments, which includes more opportunities to talk about their needs and what they want.

But as we've discussed, medical appointments don't always go the way we want them to, and sometimes you might be left feeling a bit down – especially if the conversation has been about solutions or 'fixes' that make you feel like your body or brain is A Problem. Hannah left me with some great advice for dealing with those feelings:

> *I like to remind myself of all the things I like about my disability, like my amazing disabled friends, all the different ways I've found to do things and the fact that I can support other disabled people. When people talk about 'fixing me', I just smile and say, "I'm fine just as I am, thanks" and roll away ...!*

I hope by the time you reach the end of this chapter, you feel totally comfortable about using your voice to talk to medical staff about what you need or want – or maybe when it's necessary, simply walking (or rolling) away, like Hannah. Next, we're going to talk about using your voice in a different way: being a voice for the disabled community. But before we move on, **here are some key things to remember** – whether you're in hospital, the doctor's waiting room, or having to make important medical decisions:

 Your body and brain are yours, and while healthcare professionals can give you valuable advice, **you and your adult should have the final say** when it comes to your medical care.

 You don't have to say yes to any treatment that you're not sure about straightaway. Talk about it with a trusted adult, connect with others from your disabled community to seek advice, research online and **take as much time as you need to make a decision that feels right for you**.

 Prepare for medical appointments and talk them over with your trusted adult in advance so that you can think up any questions you might have about what's going on.

Whether you have treatments or surgeries or not, and however you feel about 'fixing' your body, **you are always welcome in the disabled community**.

 You are wonderful, exactly as you are 😀

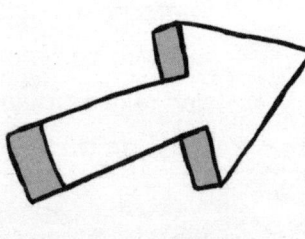
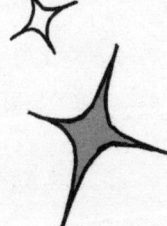

CHAPTER 8

YOU Can Help Change the World (If You Want To!)

Have you ever wanted to change the world to make it a better and more inclusive place? Perhaps you want to educate others about the issues faced by the disabled community. Well then, you definitely have what it takes to be an activist (if you fancy it).

An activist is someone who stands up for what they believe in, hoping to achieve some sort of change that improves the lives of people they care about. Activists fight for the equality and equity of people or animals who aren't treated fairly, and to try to get people in power to care about causes like the environment and climate.

Equality: when everyone is treated the same way, regardless of any differences.

Equity: when everyone is given what they need to succeed – so if they need extra support, this is provided.

Maybe you've heard of Greta Thunberg, who is one of the most famous – and youngest – climate activists in the world (and she's disabled too, by the way!). Or Martin Luther King, who fought for Black people's civil rights in the USA in the 1950s and 60s.

Some of the most famous activists throughout history were involved in protests in where they came together outside government buildings and at important landmarks before going on marches to raise awareness and gather support for the injustices going on at the time.

Protests still happen regularly but now, thanks to technology, there are more ways than ever to be an activist. There are already loads of brilliant people fighting for different causes in lots of ways, and there is *always* room for more!

DISABLED ACTIVISTS OF THE PAST AND PRESENT

A lot of things have improved for disabled people since I was a kid, and a lot of that is largely down to the awesome disabled people who have campaigned throughout history and fought hard for us to have the rights and opportunities we now enjoy. Without activists' hard work, persistence and bravery, disabled people in this country would have fewer rights and less control over their lives than we do now.

Judy Heumann (1947-2023)

Judy Heumann was an American disability rights activist who is often thought of as the 'mother' of the disability rights movement. Her work with governments and organizations – both in the United States and around the world – has helped develop and improve human-rights legislation and policies affecting disabled people. She also created Disability in Action, a group that focused on improving the rights of disabled people through protesting. But perhaps the most famous thing Judy did was in 1972, when she organized a sit-in where eighty other disability rights activists sat down on a busy road in New York City, stopping all the traffic in protest against the US president Richard Nixon's decision not to pass a law that would have benefited disabled people. The law was passed the following year, which was a huge victory for Judy and the disabled community in the USA!

Disabled People Against Cuts – DPAC (2010-present)

Disabled People Against Cuts is an activist group founded in 2010 to campaign for equality for disabled people in the UK. The group, which has over 4,000 members and many thousands more supporters, tries to get the UK government to provide the money and resources needed to support disabled people in this country through protests and actions.

Linda Burnip is one of DPAC's founders and she both organizes and goes to lots of protests. She told me that:

> It's important that disabled people are seen, and that we bring attention to issues faced by people in our community.

Shani Dhanda (1987-present)

Shani Dhanda is a British disability advocate and speaker. She travels around the world speaking to organizations and powerful people about ableism, inaccessibility and her experiences as a British-Asian disabled woman. She has won numerous awards for her work, including being awarded the title of Britain's Most Influential Disabled Person 2023 by the Shaw Trust. She also created the Asian Disability Network.

Shani, talking to me about her work, said:

> *It's incredibly rewarding to witness the changes and improvements that happen because of the information and help I provide. I also get to meet interesting people and travel to cool places around the world.*

Judy, the activists at DPAC and Shani are just a few examples of the hundreds of brilliant people who have worked hard to improve things for our community. But there's still a long road ahead to ensure disabled people have true equity today. This is great news if you're interested in becoming a disability activist, as it means there's plenty of space for you to get involved! Our community needs all the help we can get.

Linda says that being part of a protest is empowering for people who are often ignored (people like us!), and those whose words aren't taken seriously:

> *Things would be a lot worse for us if there were no protests in the past, so we keep protesting to make sure we are doing everything we can for our future.*

OTHER FORMS OF ACTIVISM

There is no perfect way to be an activist, and there are lots of different ways we can take a stand for what we believe in. If you've got the passion for making the world a better place, here are some important actions you could take part in:

⭐ **Writing to MPs and local councillors** to put pressure on them to change local and government policies that discriminate against disabled people. Ask them to support policies that would help improve issues disabled people face.

⭐ Going to events where MPs and political leaders are present – such as public debates – and **voicing your opinion** (or encouraging your adults to go on your behalf!).

⭐ Attending protest marches and demonstrations that **raise awareness** of disability issues (if you are able and the event is accessible to you).

⭐ **Helping to support other disabled people** (if they want and need it) when they face ableism and inaccessibility.

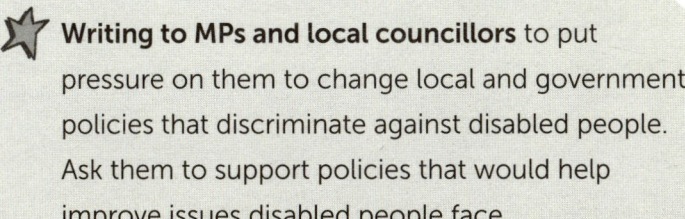

⭐ Using creative arts – such as painting, drawing, theatre or music – to **share and highlight stories** from the disabled community.

⭐ **Getting involved with actions** organized by local disability groups and organizations.

⭐ **Signing petitions** (requests made to people in power to help a group of people) that are aimed at improving the rights of disabled people and encouraging others to sign too.

⭐ Helping your school, or any other groups or organizations that you attend, to **learn about ableism and inaccessibility** and what changes can be made to better support disabled kids.

⭐ **Following and interacting** with disabled activists and disabled people on social media, and sharing their work with your friends.

⭐ **Speaking about disability, ableism and inaccessibility** wherever you feel it is appropriate and you feel comfortable doing so. And letting the world know you're disabled and proud (or at least kinda sorta okay with it)!

You don't have to do all – or any – of those things if you don't want to, of course. You might be disabled, but that doesn't mean it's your 'job' to educate others about ableism. But if you feel comfortable doing so, then using your voice can be a powerful way to engage others on accessibility issues. Simply expressing yourself and taking part in society in the ways that you enjoy is more than enough. When you add your voice to the world, whatever you decide to say and however you do it, you bring a unique perspective that is valuable and important.

You deserve to have your say on the things you care about, just like anyone else.

AWARENESS ACTIVISM

You might have celebrated a disability awareness day or month before at school or in another group or organization. This is a date every year when awareness is raised about a specific disability or group of disabilities.

It could involve sharing information at school or in the workplace, or fundraising for charities that support people with that particular disability. Dwarfism Awareness Month is in October in both the UK and the USA. Some people wear green on that day and educate others about what living with dwarfism is like.

Awareness days or months can be useful because they can help to tell people about disabilities they may not know much about, as well as raising money for important causes. But at the same time, they can be a tricky experience for some disabled kids. No disabled child should ever be made to feel like they have to explain their disability in order to receive the support they need or make people care about them.

Some disabled kids enjoy sharing about their disability and taking part in fundraising. But if this is something that doesn't feel right for you, and you're not sure how to let your school, club or organization know that you don't want to take part in an awareness day or month, then speak to a trusted adult about it. You should never be expected to talk about your disability in a way that makes you uncomfortable.

I didn't enjoy this kind of thing when I was a kid, and I still don't enjoy it now. While it's vital that disabled people have the money, equipment and support that they need, I feel strongly that those things should come from our government and people in power, not school kids, parents and local communities.

I don't think we should have to ask ordinary, individual people to give us money to help our community. That feels strange to me, and I don't want to have to explain my disability to people for that reason. I want governments and people in power to support disabled people properly with the money and access they require. Surely it's kinda sorta part of their job?!

HOW TO RESPOND WHEN YOU'RE FACED WITH ABLEISM

We've talked about how you can use activism to stand up to injustices faced by disabled people. But what about when you come face-to-face with someone who is being ableist in their words or actions? What should you do?

(*Psst* – if you need a reminder of what ableism is, it's when people are unkind to you because of the way your disability makes them feel. It's not your fault, and you don't deserve their unkindness.)

When I was in Year 4, there were these two boys who I thought were my friends, but one day they decided to team up and be mean to me. They called me a pig nose because my nose is short and goes up at the end, and they laughed at me. I felt really sad, and the teacher decided the best way to deal with that was to make the boys write me a letter of apology (which was actually kinda embarrassing). I think I still have those letters somewhere . . .

The teacher thought that making the boys feel ashamed about what they did would get them to stop being mean. But now I can see that what those boys needed was an education and an understanding that people's differences are okay and not something to make fun of.

Instead of using shame, a better approach would have been for the teacher to explain to those boys that they were being ableist, that this wasn't okay, and how they could do better. Perhaps if I wanted to, I could have even explained this to those boys myself (but in that moment, I was far too shy and sad – and that was okay too).

If you see or experience someone acting in a way that is ableist, and you feel comfortable calling them out on it, you could try gently educating them by saying one of the following things:

That was an unkind thing to say, and it hurt my feelings. Can we talk about it?

What you said just now sounded a bit ableist. Recently I've been learning about what ableism is – can I tell you a bit more about it?

I've been reading a book all about disability and why ableism is rubbish – can I show it to you? (Then you can lend them this book!)

MY JOURNEY TO ACTIVISM

A few years ago, I saw something online where a famous person was making fun of disabled people. The words they used were cruel, and it really hurt that their audience was laughing away at us too. I wrote about how it made me feel on my social media, and lots of people shared my post with others.

I continued writing about inaccessibility and ableism – from the things people can do to help to all the great things about being disabled, like having my awesome community. Before I knew it, my Instagram page had grown a following of over 30,000 people, which is about the size of a medium-sized town, and even included some famous people! (Still no Beyoncé yet, though ☹)

Editors of newspapers and magazines contacted me and asked me to write articles about disability discrimination and representation in film and TV.

Then organizations started asking me to speak at conferences and events, and then authors asked me to contribute chapters about ableism and discrimination to their books.

Now I've written my own book – this one! Wow!

I really enjoy talking about ableism, inaccessibility and disability representation, and sharing parts of my story. I don't share what it's like having dwarfis; I share what it's like living in a world that sometimes doesn't accept people with dwarfism.

While it can be difficult sometimes – especially when people don't 'get it' or are purposefully mean – when I receive messages from people saying I've helped them to understand things better, I know it's worth it. People have also told me they feel better prepared to talk about these things with their families thanks to my work (as well as the work of lots of other cool people – there's a list at the end of this book!). But the kind of feedback I love more than anything is when other disabled people tell me that they have felt more encouraged and less alone after reading or hearing my words.

Lots of disabled people, like me, are born into families with no direct experience of our disabilities, and it can be super lonely facing life's challenges with nobody alongside us who understands our unique experiences. But thanks to social media, TV, film, radio, music and the internet, it's now so much easier to find similar stories to our own and to form a community with others like us. I sometimes felt very alone as a kid, but I think if young me had existed in today's connected world, my experience would have been totally different.

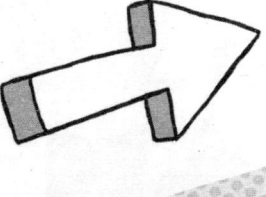

YOU'RE GOING TO CHANGE THE WORLD

Activism can be about any injustice – disabled people are just one of the communities we can fight for. There are incredible activist movements around the world focused on tackling issues such as racism, the refugee crisis, LGBTQAI+ rights, environmental issues and more. For me, I love writing and I love my disabled community, so it felt natural to combine my skills and experience to help highlight the issues that we face and hopefully make a difference. I also support lots of other activist groups by joining in with and sharing the work they're doing when I can.

Even if one person feels more educated or changes their mind about an issue or a community group, that's something. After all, you never know how far your words will go ...

DISABILITY RIGHTS

Shani agrees, and she shared some advice with me for anyone wanting to get into disability activism or advocacy:

Learn about the history of the disability rights movement and the people involved, and find out what issues matter to you. Activism can include expressing your opinions, joining protests, educating others, or making art for change. Connect with other activists and groups, start small and take care of yourself along the way.
You've got this!

Throughout history, the loudest voices and best-known stories tend to be from the people with the most money, privilege and power, and not many of those people are disabled.

? **Privilege:** the advantage(s) someone or a group of people has because their identity may mean they are less likely to be discriminated against. Everyone has different privileges – I have privileges due to being white, British and because I went to university, for example.

But those aren't the only stories that need to be told. **We all have an important story.** What's yours?

Activism isn't
about being
the 'hero' of
a community.

It's about working
together with
others to create
real change.

If you're interested in activism now or in the future, here are **some important reminders from this chapter...**

 Educate yourself. Keep up to date with events in the news that affect disability rights and learn about the history of the disability rights movement (as Shani recommends!). The more you know, the more you'll feel ready to speak to others about disability rights issues. **Knowledge is power!**

 Speak up. Whether that's in the classroom, at home or in clubs or organizations that you're part of, sharing your thoughts and educating others about disability discrimination can be a powerful tool towards creating change.

 Remember, we're stronger together. Connecting with the disabled community – whether online or in person – can strengthen our activism and means we're more likely to be heard. Activism isn't about being the 'hero' of a community. It's about working together with others to create real change.

 Every action counts. You don't have to do ALL the things suggested in this chapter to be an activist or to fight for change. Life is busy enough as it is! If you can only do a couple of things every now and again – that's fantastic. The more voices that are in the disability rights movement, the better.

CHAPTER 9

The World of Work

(Gah! We're Talking About That Already?!)

Do you know what you'd like to be when you grow up? I know that question can be kinda sorta annoying sometimes. How are you supposed to know what job you want to do as an adult when you're still a kid? And what about if you're unsure if the world of work is right for you? Or maybe you're worried about exactly *how* you'll be able to do the job of your dreams?

Okay, firstly I want to say that it is *totally fine* if you don't know what job you want to do when you're older, or if you don't want to do one at all. I had no idea that I would end up doing what I do now, and I love it! Plus, it's way more common now for people to change jobs throughout their life – you don't have to stick to just one thing. Follow your heart, or however the cheesy saying goes.

Secondly, and more importantly, the world of work *can* and *should* be open to you. Many disabled people are, and can be, teachers, artists, inventors, doctors, lawyers, gardeners, chefs, carers, mechanics, secretaries, managers, singers, celebrities and, well, lots of other jobs. There are actually very few professions that are impossible for most of us to do – they might just require some adaptations and perhaps some work colleagues with a more open and flexible mindset. (Although I'm pretty gutted people with dwarfism

aren't allowed to be astronauts – give me a space suit please, I want to bounce around in zero gravity!)

Of course, I should also mention here that some disabled people are unable to work. It's really important that disabled people are supported whether they are able to or want to work, or not. People who can't work or don't want to aren't any less important or valuable than those who can.

It's also worth saying that just because you're disabled, it does not mean you have to work in something disability related. Not everyone wants to be an activist or talk about the issues their communities face all the time – sometimes it feels really nice to work in an area that's nothing to do with that stuff. I really love my disability-related work, but I often get frustrated when people think I do that because it's the only job I or other disabled people can do. We can be, and do, anything we want to, *thank you very much* (and if we want to do not very much at all, that's totally fine too!).

I know getting a job might feel like it's AGES away – but it can be useful to hear about the wide range of jobs that are available to you, and to learn about the experiences of disabled people who are in work so that you can feel empowered to make decisions about your career in the future. But before we talk about that, I have a question for you...

Do you know what links all these people?

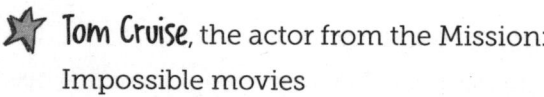 **Tom Cruise**, the actor from the Mission: Impossible movies

 **Stephen Hawking**, the scientist

 **Daniel Radcliffe**, the actor who played Harry Potter

 **Frida Kahlo**, very successful artist – she's the one with the cool monobrow!

Stevie Wonder, musician

Selena Gomez, actress and singer

Justin Timberlake, singer and actor

See opposite for the answer!

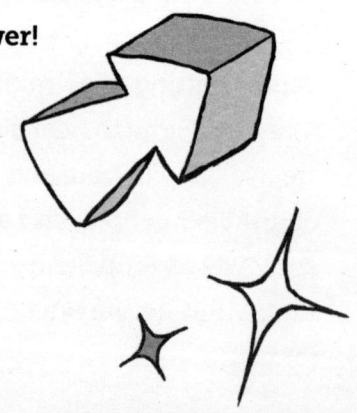

226

They're all REALLY famous, and they're all disabled.

⭐ **Tom Cruise** has dyslexia

⭐ **Stephen Hawking** had ALS, also known as motor neurone disease, and was a wheelchair user

⭐ **Daniel Radcliffe** has dyspraxia

⭐ **Frida Kahlo** had spina bifida and, later, polio

⭐ **Stevie Wonder** is blind

⭐ **Selena Gomez** has lupus

⭐ **Justin Timberlake** has ADHD

Bet you didn't know half those people were disabled, right? That's just the tip of the iceberg too – loads of famous people are disabled! And seeing people like us being successful at what they do proves that we can also be whatever we want to be. All we need sometimes is for the world to catch up and realize we're as capable as we say we are.

FIRST JOBS

I'm guessing that if you're reading this, then you probably haven't started working yet (if that's something you can and want to do). But maybe you have an older sibling or friend who does. Getting a first job when you're a teenager teaches you important stuff like how to manage your time and how to work as part of a team, and of course, the best bit is that you get to earn your own money to use however you want!

I got my first job when I was sixteen. I was so excited to be able to have my own money that I had worked to earn. My first job was at a Budgens supermarket, where I worked on the checkouts every Sunday. I had a step under the checkout for my feet and was allowed to sit down while I scanned people's shopping because standing up was painful if I did it for too long. Plus, sometimes people couldn't see me over their shopping!

Most of the time I really enjoyed my job. People – especially old ladies – were usually up for a good chat as their shopping passed through the checkout, and I got to know so many familiar faces from around town. Having people smile at me and ask how I was all day was lovely! When I couldn't reach their shopping or it was too heavy, people were also usually all too willing to help. The hours were long though, and I often got tired sitting at the checkout – the seat I had wasn't very good at supporting my spine, so my back used to hurt a lot. As a teenager, I just wanted to blend in and use the same stuff as everyone else. I could have asked for adaptations, but sometimes I didn't want to.

When you get to the age where you might want to go out and get your first job, it can be useful to have a think about the sort of environment you'd like to work in, and the kinds of adaptations you might need – just like we talked about when preparing for secondary school. There's actually a law (the same Equality Act 2010 we mentioned in Chapter 3) that says workplaces have to provide the adaptations and support needed for you to do your job. Here are some things that in future you might want to think about:

What will I need in the workplace to be able to do my job?

This could be anything from a supportive chair to noise-cancelling headphones, a computer screen for visually impaired people or transport to and from work. You'll be the expert in what you need.

Do I need anything different to what workplaces usually offer their employees?

For example, the ability to take breaks when you need to or more time off.

What should I tell my workplace to help them understand how to support me?

You don't have to share everything about your disabilities but if you think you'll need support in your job, it might help if you tell them your access needs.

Can I *really* do most jobs?

Well, probably, but only you know that! It's likely there will be a mix – some jobs you can't do, some jobs you'd need adaptations to do, and some jobs that are more accessible to you.

Balancing finding a job you care about that also meets your access needs can be tricky at times. If, when you're a bit older, you feel a bit stuck thinking about all that stuff, talking to a careers advisor and other disabled people you know might help you to figure it out. Just remember that whether or not you end up with your dream job, you are a special and valuable person and the world is lucky to have you.

DISABILITY DISCRIMINATION AT WORK (BOO)

Although things are much better now than when I was starting out in the world of work, ableism in the workplace sadly still exists. In this book so far, we've talked about how different systems – such as the education system and the medical system – can be inaccessible to us, and the world of work is another. This could be because an office hasn't been designed to be accessible – maybe the desks are too close together to allow a wheelchair to pass through, for example. It could also be to do with people's attitudes, such as assuming a disabled colleague won't be able to do certain things without actually asking them.

I first experienced discrimination at work when I applied for a job at a fancy London department store in my second year of university. I was invited to a group interview, where everyone who wanted a job sat in a room together. I was the only person in that room (I think) who was physically disabled, and everyone else was wearing high heels and make-up. They looked so glamorous. When it came to my turn to speak, I was spoken to really rudely by the people interviewing me. A week later, a letter arrived in the post saying that I didn't get the job. It didn't say why, but I think it was because they didn't want someone who looked like me working there.

I was really sad about my interview experience at the time. But you know what? **It was their loss.** I was a really hardworking colleague and someone that was fun to be around. My disability didn't make me any worse at my job than anyone else; it just meant I had to do things a bit differently sometimes, and most people didn't mind that at all.

After a while, I dusted myself off and tried again. I didn't let one negative experience stop me from going after what I wanted. In the interviews I had after that, I noticed the way the people treated me before deciding whether I wanted to work for them. That helped me to remember that **getting a job wasn't just their decision, it was mine too.**

You deserve to find interesting, fun and rewarding work if you want to, just like everyone else. It might feel scary to even try going for a job you really want because it just sounds too impossible. But like anything in life, **you'll never know until you try.** Sometimes as disabled people we will encounter barriers to finding work, or even once we've got the job we want, we find that the workplace isn't particularly accessible. But this isn't something we just have to accept – we can advocate for change too. The good news is that a lot of work is being done behind the scenes to make workplaces more accessible – for example, many bigger companies and workplaces have disability networks, which campaign for the improvement of working conditions for disabled people.

UNLOCKING YOUR PASSION

If you can find something that you feel really passionate about doing, then work doesn't have to feel like work – at least not all the time, anyway! I have always enjoyed writing, but when I was younger, I never realized that I could make money from it. After university, I managed to find a really cool job working in music, which I loved, and after that I kicked off my career in writing and editing. Finally, I had found my 'thing' – something I felt confident doing, that I could access, and that I really enjoyed! If I could go back in time and tell twelve-year-old me that in the future I'd be an editor and a writer, younger me would never have believed it.

What are your special skills or interests? Maybe you're really into film, or photography, or football? Have you ever thought about pursuing your favourite thing as a career? That might feel like an impossible dream, but I promise it can come true for you.

I spoke to the author Elle McNicoll all about how she turned her passion into a career. Elle writes magical books, such as *A Kind Of Spark*, all about characters who also happen to be neurodivergent, like she is. Putting neurodivergent characters front and centre of her stories is such a brilliant way of showing the world that neurodivergence is a normal part of our society.

I asked Elle how she became a writer, and she said:

> *I worked a lot as a professional actor when I was a child ... but I wanted to create my own stories, rather than perform other people's. I had (and still have!) a huge imagination and I loved reading books. Those two elements definitely collided and made me start writing stories, usually backstage or between rehearsals and shows. I much preferred writing stories to homework!*

She also shared some fantastic advice for anyone who might feel unsure about following their career dreams:

One, I think it's really important to be your own best friend. You deserve the things you want to achieve in life, just as much as everyone else.

Two, failure is never as terrible as regret, so give yourself a chance and take risks! Especially when it comes to the things you dream about.

Three, never let any other person's negative words become the voice in your head. I never need easy; I just need possible. So even if it's hard, keep going.

And four – always remember: You are more than enough!

I found Elle's words really encouraging and they can apply to lots of different parts of life, not just work. Achieving the things we want isn't always easy, but if we focus on what's possible then we can get there – even if it takes us a long time or we have to deal with people doubting us.

DEFYING EXPECTATIONS

Having people say 'no' and think you can't do things is really rubbish, especially when you know you can. Sometimes non-disabled people expect us not to be able to do stuff just because we're disabled, when often the only thing holding us back is their negative attitudes. Someone who knows all about overcoming people's expectations is Simon Wheatcroft. Simon lost his sight at seventeen years old, but in many ways that's when his life truly started:

> When I became blind, I felt lost for a while. The number of blind people who were in work or in relationships was low.

But Simon didn't give up – people telling him he couldn't do things only made him want to prove them wrong:

> I realized that those numbers tell us where we are, not where we can go.

Simon was so determined to push the boundaries of what people thought of him that he decided to train to become a long-distance runner, and after spending seven months training, he ran his first ever race – a cool 100 miles!

Since then, Simon has hung up his running shoes and can now be found in the classroom – yes, he's a teacher. It took him a while to find people who were willing to train a Blind person to be a teacher, but once he did, he quickly passed his course and began his new career:

> *I had to stop thinking, 'What do others think of me?', and instead think, 'What do I want to do?', and just go for it.*

In his first year of teaching, he won a national teaching award! Simon is a fantastic example of someone who didn't let other people's expectations hold him back from doing what he wanted to do:

> *From struggling to find an organization to train me to winning a teaching award – my journey proves that achieving your goals is absolutely possible. You just have to find people who are willing to support you on that journey.*

WHY REPRESENTATION MATTERS

When I was a kid, it was extremely rare to see people who looked like me on TV, in films or in books. Now, we're everywhere! Well okay, not quite, but lots of us are doing cool things. It's so important to see other disabled people living out their dream careers, because it helps us to know that the dreams we have are possible too.

Cara Mailey is a fifteen-year-old mixed race girl with dwarfism. Despite her young age, she's already been on TV (including *Blue Peter* and *Derry Girls*), released her own accessible clothing range and even written a book! *I Got This* is a brilliant story about a girl with dwarfism navigating teenage life. Of all the things she's achieved, Cara told me her favourite was creating that story.

> *The best thing was writing a book with a main character not only having a disability, but **my** disability! Erin [the character in I Got This] has my skin colour and achondroplasia. I was able to put so many aspects of my life into it and teach others. I love seeing it in the shops still today!*

Cara loves our big dwarfism community and goes to loads of dwarfism events in Ireland and in the UK every year. She says being part of this network has helped her to feel proud to be disabled:

> I think it's important to be proud. That's not easy though, I know – but that's why I think it's important to have friends and others in my life who have dwarfism.

For a girl that's achieved so much already, she still has some pretty big dreams:

> I'd love to be in a musical in the West End. I know of two other people with dwarfism that have been on the West End. It's not common, I know, and I'm setting the bar high – but who knows?

Judging by how much she's accomplished at such a young age, I wouldn't be surprised if I saw Cara in the West End in the next few years at all.

OVER TO YOU!

If you are someone who wants to work in the future, what do you want to do? Are you interested in teaching like Simon, writing like Elle, acting like Cara, working in shops like I once did, or maybe something completely different? Would you like to be famous for what you do, or would you prefer that most people don't know who you are? Do you want to do a job that is linked to disability? Or maybe something completely unrelated, maybe a bit of lots of things, or maybe nothing at all.

Write down your answers below if you want to. You could look back at them in a year or so and check whether you feel the same!

WORK WORK WORK WORK WORK . . . (ISN'T THAT WHAT RIHANNA SAID?)

Before we move on, let's remember a few important things:

 It can be cool thinking about the things **you really enjoy** and the jobs that are linked to them.

 It's also totally cool not to know what you want to do in the future, or to feel like you don't want to work at all, or if you can't work. Work certainly isn't everything – so long as you're happy, that's what's most important.

 It's awesome if you want to do a job that's related to disability somehow, but you absolutely don't have to do that just because you're disabled. **What excites you and makes you want to do more of it?** And what jobs are linked to it?

 Though ableism in the workplace still exists, there are so many amazing workplaces out there that want to hire disabled people and support their disabled staff. It's important to find colleagues and a work environment that make you feel good – **you deserve to be there just as much as anyone else!**

⭐ If you want to work in the future, it's **likely you can do most jobs** – you just might have to have some conversations with the people in charge to let them know what adaptations you might need.

⭐ **You are awesome** and you deserve to be able to try out whatever you want to do, to change your mind, to experiment, to have breaks when you need them and to love your work!

CHAPTER 10

Disabled and Proud
(Or at Least Kinda Sorta Okay With It)

WOWZERS – we're nearly at the end of the book and we've covered loads, from navigating school and work, friendships to family and more. We've learned about some tough stuff like inaccessibility and ableism, and how being disabled can mean we face more challenges than our non-disabled peers. But as I hope you've learned through reading this book, being disabled can be kinda sorta awesome too.

Don't believe me? If you're not convinced by now, what if I told you that being disabled means you get cool stuff? And much more importantly, that it means you get to be a super-awesome person. You get things like...

Community

Being disabled means we get to be part of a big, welcoming community of people, many of whom will have similar life experiences to you. Some of them might look like you or have a brain/body that works like yours does, and they may even share your interests and hobbies. In the disabled community you'll find plenty of love and acceptance, because everyone knows what it's like to be disabled and to be treated differently.

Life experience

Sometimes you might go through tough stuff as a disabled kid, and even as a disabled adult. Although this can be a bit rubbish, the hard times also help us to gain strength and a thicker skin, and to learn how to use our voice. They also build our compassion and empathy for others (more on those in a sec), which are qualities that no amount of money can buy.

Gadgets

Most of us disabled people have some kind of special technology we use – whether it's a mobility scooter, a powered wheelchair like Dom, a funky cane like Joy, a bed that moves up and down, a special pen or, like me, one of those fancy toilets that washes your bum! There are loads of mobility aids and adaptations that are both incredibly useful and very cool.

When I was in primary school, I once needed to use a wheelchair for a school trip, and when I wasn't using it I got to pick which friends could have a go on it. I also remember getting a ride when we had to go on long walks and choosing a mate to come with me – everyone wanted to be my friend then! These perks gave me confidence as a kid because they allowed me to access the same things as everyone else, with the added bonus of impressing my friends. (I still have a bum-washing toilet today, and I love showing it off to everyone!)

Free tickets!!!

A lot of disabled people are able to get a free ticket for a friend or carer to come with them to different kinds of events and experiences[4] – for example a concert, festival, the theatre or a museum exhibition. Taylor Swift? Legoland? The cinema?! The possibilities are endless. Now for the hard part – choosing who gets to come with you …

The life skills that you learn as a disabled person help you to be:

Empathetic and patient

Because we know what it's like to be slower at things, or to need things to be done differently, disabled people tend to be more empathetic, patient and kind towards others.

Really good at saying 'no'!

As we've explored throughout this book, disabled people often have to get comfortable with saying no. No, I don't

---

4. Once you've decided where you want to go, your parent/carer will need to investigate how to get a companion ticket beforehand, as it might mean they need to fill in a form or provide some information.

want to answer that; no I can't; no, thank you; or simply just 'no'. Two letters, one full stop – it's a full sentence!

Accepting

Again, because our bodies and minds work differently to others, disabled people are generally more accepting of other people's differences, whatever they might be.

Self-aware

Disabled people often have really good self-awareness (in other words, knowing yourself well). We have to become good at knowing our limits, setting boundaries and understanding how things affect us. We're experts in our own disabled brains and bodies, and that's very cool!

Adaptable

If there's one thing we're brilliant at, it's adapting. Because we've had to learn how to access and use things that weren't made for us, we're used to having to think of smart ways to adapt so that we can do things and have fun! That skill is super useful in all areas of life. If we're adaptable, it means we're open to finding new ways the world can work, and most of the time we get to learn something new about ourselves along the way too.

So you're adaptable, patient, empathetic, accepting, and you know both your boundaries and a thing or two about life. Sounds like you're already one awesome human being! But hey, don't just take my word for it – my mate Nina, who we heard from in Chapter 1, is back with an important message too:

> *Living a disabled life can be challenging, sometimes really challenging. But you know that amazing feeling you get when you complete a tricky level in a video game? That's the same feeling you'll get when you overcome the challenges that life can bring up. The most brilliant, interesting, funny, ingenious, and creative people I know are ALL disabled and I know you're brilliant too.*

Yes, Nina! Sometimes it can feel like we have so many challenges to get through – and sometimes they crop up at the most inconvenient times! But those challenges also help us to become brilliant at getting through difficult stuff and having a go at this weird little thing we call life.

DISABLED AND PROUD (OR AT LEAST KINDA SORTA OKAY WITH IT)

You get to decide who you are and what you bring to the world – nobody else can decide that for you. People might have their opinions, but you don't have to take any notice of them! As my pal Katouche says:

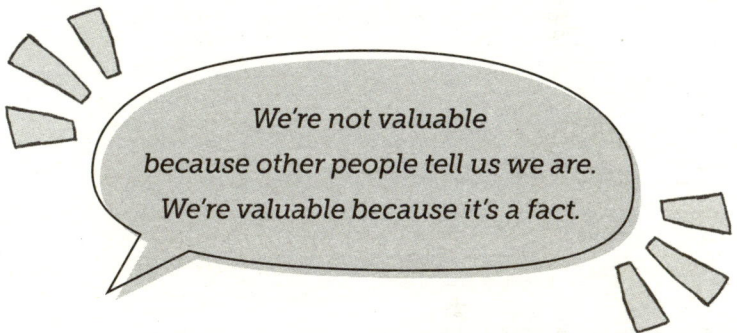

We're not valuable because other people tell us we are. We're valuable because it's a fact.

Your value doesn't depend on being able to run fast, get good grades or wear certain clothes. You are valuable because you are YOU.

We've almost reached the end of the book, and I hope it's helped in your journey to figuring out your disabled identity. In a world where being disabled can sometimes mean we are treated unfairly, and we have to make extra effort to access the same things as everyone else, it's totally normal to struggle with feeling proud of your disabled-ness from time to time.

But no matter what particular challenges and barriers you face, I want you to remember that **you are special and important, exactly the way you are.**

My journey to being proud to be disabled looks a bit like this:

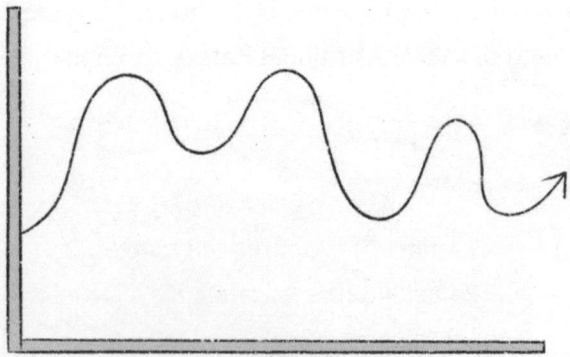

I have good days and bad days and in-between days too. Sometimes I'm really proud and sometimes I feel like I need a break. How about yours?

I find it difficult to always be proud, because sometimes ableism and inaccessibility can be hard to deal with, and it's normal to feel frustrated by that. But I am mostly okay with my disabled identity, and sometimes proud of it. I love my disabled friends – some of whom are featured in the pages of this book – and I love how being disabled has helped shape who I am. By the way, I'm kinda sorta fantastic – and I bet you are too!

GLOSSARY

All these terms feature throughout the book, but I thought it might be useful to put them here for you to refer to as well.

Please note: language changes over time – these words and definitions are all true and great to use at the time of writing, but may change later, so please check if you're unsure.

ableism
Prejudice and discrimination towards disabled people. Some people are more ableist than others, but everyone is ableist sometimes – even disabled people! That's because we are all raised in a society that sees disability as a problem, and it can take a long time for us to realize all the ways that's not true.

accessible
Something that is accessible means you can use or do it. For example, a wheelchair user might find a building entrance accessible because it has a ramp, or a Blind person might find a book accessible because it's available in audio form or Braille.

adaptation
A change that needs to be made to something – a space, an activity, a gadget – so that it is accessible for you.

anxiety
Anxiety, or being anxious, is how we feel when our tummies are all wobbly inside and we are very worried about one particular thing or lots of things. Anxiety might cause us not to sleep very well, to be extra grumpy or shy, or to act differently to how we do normally.

apparent disability
A disability we can recognize when we meet or communicate with someone.

boundaries

Limits that we set for ourselves and in our relationships with others that enable us to say 'no' to things that we don't want to – or can't – do.

burnout

We experience burnout when our bodies and minds have been working too hard for too long, often resulting in us being extremely tired and/or getting sick, and being unable to do regular activities until we slow down and look after ourselves a bit more gently.

consent

Consent is something we give when we give permission for someone else to do something. For example, you might say yes – or give your consent – when you visit the doctor with a sore throat, and they ask if they can examine your tongue.

discrimination

Discrimination means treating a person or group of people unfairly based on their characteristics.

dysphoria

Dysphoria is a sense of unhappiness with life. For people who experience gender dysphoria, this can mean they feel unhappy with the gender the world tells them they are.

empathy

The ability to understand someone else's feelings by imagining what it would be like to be in that person's situation.

equality

Equality means everyone is treated the same way, regardless of any differences.

equity

Equity means everyone is given what they need to succeed – so if they need specialized or more support, this is provided.

genderfluid

Having a gender identity that can shift and change at any time.

gene/genetic

A part of a cell that is passed down from a birth parent to a child and which controls a characteristic of your brain and/or body. Genetic describes something that is caused by your genes.

inaccessible

Something that is inaccessible means you can't use or do it – for example, I find monkey bars inaccessible because my arms are not strong enough to swing from. Someone else might find a classroom inaccessible because there are no low chairs or laptops available, or there is no one-to-one support or an induction loop (and so on).

intersectional

A way of explaining the many things that make up who we are. Someone whose identity is intersectional may be discriminated against in more than one way, whether that's through their disability, race, gender, sexuality, class, nationality or something else.

masking

Masking is something many neurodivergent, chronically ill and disabled people do sometimes when we want to fit into an environment where we feel it isn't safe for us to be ourselves. When we mask, we might be hiding our mood, our emotions, our stimming, or simply how hard the situation is for us. Masking is hiding our true selves, which can take a lot of effort and it can be very tiring.

the medical model

The medical model of disability believes that the way our bodies are – like being in pain or having a broken leg – makes our lives more challenging. It sees our bodies as the problem, and not the world around us. The medical model focuses on finding fixes and cures for our bodies.

mobility aid

A tool that a disabled person uses to help them move around, such as a wheelchair, cane or crutches.

neurodivergent

A term used to describe someone whose brain processes information in a different way to other people, which means that they face different challenges to people who are neurotypical.

neurotypical

A term used to describe someone whose brain functions in the way that is expected, or considered 'normal'.

non-apparent disability

A disability we cannot recognize when we meet or communicate with someone.

non-binary
Having a gender identity that isn't male or female.

othering
When you other someone, you treat them like they're not part of your group because they're different in some way. This can be experienced by anyone, not just disabled kids, but it can often happen to disabled kids more.

prejudice
Holding certain beliefs about a person based on their characteristics.

privilege
Privilege is the advantage(s) someone or a group of people has because their identity holds more power, and they are less discriminated against. Everyone has different privileges – I have privileges due to being white, British and because I've been to university, for example.

queer
A term describing any sexual orientation and/or gender identity that may fall outside the common types. Some people use 'queer' to describe anyone in the LGBTQAI+ community – but it's always best to check what term people prefer.

sensory overload
When one or more of your five senses (touch, sight, hearing, smell and taste) are overwhelmed with too much information and create more feelings than you can handle.

shame
The sadness or embarrassment we feel when we realize or are told something we have done is wrong or bad. When someone shames someone else, it means they say or do things to make them feel bad for what they have done.

the social model
The social model of disability is used to describe how things that happen outside of our bodies, like people being unkind and the world not being accessible, make our lives more challenging. It sees society as the problem. The social model focuses on trying to educate the world and make it a more accommodating and inclusive place.

solidarity
Support between two or more people because they share the same feelings, aims or identity.

Special Educational Needs Co-ordinator (SENCO)

Every school has someone called a SENCO, whose job it is to support kids who have special educational needs. This support is available between the ages of five and fifteen in England. Some of the things a SENCO does are tell your parents or carer about any needs you have if they don't already know, help you find the right support, equipment and adaptations you need at school and talk to your healthcare providers about your changing needs.

white supremacy

The system our world runs on, which believes that white people are better than Black, Brown and Indigenous people, and other marginalized groups, and should have power over them. It is a system that places rich, slim, white, non-disabled people as most valuable and most important, and everyone else beneath them.

KINDA SORTA PRETTY AWESOME DISABLED PEOPLE

All the people listed below have helped to shape me and countless others – whether that's through educating us, entertaining us, fighting for our rights or just being fantastic examples of wonderful disabled people who have had a positive impact on the world. There's never one person who represents a community – we all do. But these are just some of the people I think do this for the disabled community in a really cool way.

My kinda sorta pretty awesome disabled icons:

Ade Adepitan, children's TV presenter and wheelchair basketball player.

Alice Wong, activist. Alice founded the Disability Visibility Project, an important piece of work which collects interviews from disabled people telling parts of history.

Fats Timbo, comedian, model and author. Her TikToks are hilarious!

Francesca Martinez, comedian, theatre and TV actor. Francesca has been in some of the funniest shows I've ever watched.

Frances Ryan, journalist and author. Frances writes about the issues disabled people face in the UK for the newspaper the *Guardian*.

Imani Barbarin, writer and public speaker. Imani makes really informative, easy-to-understand videos about disability politics in the US.

James and **Lucy Catchpole**, authors of the kids' books *What Happened To You?*, *You're So Amazing* and *Mama Car*, which all feature positive and uplifting disabled stories.

John Pring, editor of Disability News Service, a website dedicated to providing news on disability issues across the UK.

Saida Ahmed, comedian and actor. Saida always brings fun and comedy to her performances!

Wednesday Holmes, queer artist, author and illustrator. Wednesday's illustrations always help me to feel loved and put me in a great mood.

Yayoi Kusama, artist specializing in modern pop art. Yayoi's famous exhibit Infinity Rooms has been installed in galleries all over the world.

KINDA SORTA PRETTY AWESOME BOOKS

Are any of these in your school or local library? If they're not, could you ask them whether they can order some copies in?

Fiction

A Kind Of Spark, Keedie, Like a Charm, Show Us Who You Are and *Some Like It Cold*, by Elle McNicoll. Fantasy reads starring neurodivergent main characters.

All The Things That Could Go Wrong by Stewart Foster. A story about what happens when two boys, one of whom has OCD, have to put aside their differences.

The Amazing Edie Eckhart series by Rosie Jones. A fun set of stories about the adventures of a girl with cerebral palsy.

An Alien in the Jam Factory by Chrissie Sains. The first book in an adventure series about Scooter the inventor, who has cerebral palsy, and his top-secret alien sidekick.

Cosima Unfortunate Steals A Star by Laura Noakes. An exciting adventure story featuring a group of disabled kids.

El Deafo by Cece Bell. A comic about a rabbit human and their experiences wearing a hearing aid for the first time, inspired by the author's life.

I Got This by Chrissie Sains and Cara Mailey. A novel about a young mixed-race girl with achondroplasia dwarfism trying to navigate the world.

Ink Girls by Marieke Nijkamp. An energetic graphic novel with a neurodivergent main character who uses a cane.

Marcelene, Defender of the Sea by Jen Campbell. A story about a child who has to miss a school trip because they need to go into hospital for an operation.

Vivi Conway and the Sword of Legend by Lizzie Huxley-Jones. A swashbuckling story about how it feels to be autistic while trying to save the world.

Non-fiction

A Different Sort Of Normal by Abigail Balfe. A wonderful, fun and informative book for older kids about growing up with autism.

A Kids Book About Disability by Kristine Napper. A really helpful starting point on how to talk about disability.

Allies by multiple authors. A book with lots of authors detailing great ways to support people of many identities.

Bless the Blood by Walela Nehanda. A memoir for teens about Walela's experiences as a Black cancer patient.

Everyday Action, Everyday Change by Natalie and Naomi Evans. A book about how to change the world through small actions. I contributed a small part about disability activism to this book!

Not All Heroes Wear Capes by Jono Lancaster. A book about Jono's journey to finding happiness as a person with a facial difference.

Unmasked: The Ultimate Guide to Autism, ADHD and Neurodivergence by Ellie Middleton. An accessible, information-packed guide to neurodivergence and finding your place in the world.

Wonderfully Wired Brains: An Introduction to the World of Neurodiversity by Louise Gooding. An informative book explaining neurodiversity and how our brains work.

ORGANIZATIONS AND RESOURCES

These websites might be useful for your parent/carer, if they want to find out anything or keep up to date with things going on in the community.

Contact. Offers free support for families of disabled *children.*
www.contact.org.uk

Council for Disabled Children. A network offering advice and advocating for the rights of disabled children in the UK.
www. councilfordisabledchildren.org.uk

Disability Living Allowance (DLA). Money given to the families of disabled children to help pay for things they need.
www.gov.uk/disability-living-allowance-children

Disability News Service. Providing news for and about disabled people in the UK.
www.disabilitynewsservice.com

Disabled People Against Cuts. A group of disabled people across the UK who advocate for change.
www.dpac.uk.net

Family Fund. A charity providing financial aid and support for families with disabled children.

www.familyfund.com

Mermaids. A charity supporting transgender and non-binary adults and children in the UK.

www.mermaidsuk.org.uk

Period Positivity Movement. A website explaining the movement and how you can get involved.

www.periodpositive.com

Scope. A charity supporting disabled people in the UK.

www.scope.org

The Hub. Offers support and advice for young disabled people.

www.hub.kids.org.uk

ACKNOWLEDGEMENTS

With thanks to the people interviewed in the book:
Jameisha Prescod, Ellie Middleton, Nina Tame, Ivy Broadhead, Junior Bishop, Lorna McFindlow, Ellie Simmonds, Joy Addo, Rico Cox, Max Fisher, Katouche Goll, Dom Hyams, Hannah Barham-Brown, Linda Burnip, Shani Dhanda, Elle McNicoll, Simon Wheatcroft and Cara Mailey.

Special thanks also go to Jaleel Hudson for her fabulous illustrations, my mum and dad, my agent Megan Staunton, Meg Osborne, my editor at Puffin, and all the disabled people, past, present and future, who pave the way for us all.